# TIMON OF AT

## William Shake

# ACT I

## SCENE I. Athens. A hall in Timon's house.

*Enter Poet, Painter, Jeweller, Merchant, and others, at several doors*

Poet

Good day, sir.

Painter

I am glad you're well.

Poet

I have not seen you long: how goes the world?

Painter

It wears, sir, as it grows.

Poet

Ay, that's well known:

But what particular rarity? what strange,

Which manifold record not matches? See,

Magic of bounty! all these spirits thy power

Hath conjured to attend. I know the merchant.

Painter

I know them both; th' other's a jeweller.

Merchant

O, 'tis a worthy lord.

Jeweller

Nay, that's most fix'd.

Merchant

A most incomparable man, breathed, as it were,

To an untirable and continuate goodness:

He passes.

Jeweller: I have a jewel here--

Merchant

O, pray, let's see't: for the Lord Timon, sir?

Jeweller: If he will touch the estimate: but, for that--

Poet

[Reciting to himself] 'When we for recompense have

praised the vile,

It stains the glory in that happy verse

Which aptly sings the good.'

Merchant

'Tis a good form.

Looking at the jewel

Jeweller

And rich: here is a water, look ye.

Painter

You are rapt, sir, in some work, some dedication

To the great lord.

**Poet**

A thing slipp'd idly from me.

Our poesy is as a gum, which oozes

From whence 'tis nourish'd: the fire i' the flint

Shows not till it be struck; our gentle flame

Provokes itself and like the current flies

Each bound it chafes. What have you there?

**Painter**

A picture, sir. When comes your book forth?

**Poet**

Upon the heels of my presentment, sir.

Let's see your piece.

**Painter**

'Tis a good piece.

**Poet**

So 'tis: this comes off well and excellent.

**Painter**

Indifferent.

**Poet**

Admirable: how this grace

Speaks his own standing! what a mental power

This eye shoots forth! how big imagination

Moves in this lip! to the dumbness of the gesture

One might interpret.

**Painter**

It is a pretty mocking of the life.

Here is a touch; is't good?

Poet

I will say of it,

It tutors nature: artificial strife

Lives in these touches, livelier than life.

*Enter certain Senators, and pass over*

Painter

How this lord is follow'd!

Poet

The senators of Athens: happy man!

Painter

Look, more!

Poet

You see this confluence, this great flood

of visitors.

I have, in this rough work, shaped out a man,

Whom this beneath world doth embrace and hug

With amplest entertainment: my free drift

Halts not particularly, but moves itself

In a wide sea of wax: no levell'd malice

Infects one comma in the course I hold;

But flies an eagle flight, bold and forth on,

Leaving no tract behind.

Painter

How shall I understand you?

Poet

I will unbolt to you.

You see how all conditions, how all minds,

As well of glib and slippery creatures as

Of grave and austere quality, tender down

Their services to Lord Timon: his large fortune

Upon his good and gracious nature hanging

Subdues and properties to his love and tendance

All sorts of hearts; yea, from the glass-faced flatterer

To Apemantus, that few things loves better

Than to abhor himself: even he drops down

The knee before him, and returns in peace

Most rich in Timon's nod.

Painter

I saw them speak together.

Poet

Sir, I have upon a high and pleasant hill

Feign'd Fortune to be throned: the base o' the mount

Is rank'd with all deserts, all kind of natures,

That labour on the bosom of this sphere

To propagate their states: amongst them all,

Whose eyes are on this sovereign lady fix'd,

One do I personate of Lord Timon's frame,

Whom Fortune with her ivory hand wafts to her;

Whose present grace to present slaves and servants

Translates his rivals.

Painter

'Tis conceived to scope.

This throne, this Fortune, and this hill, methinks,

With one man beckon'd from the rest below,

Bowing his head against the sleepy mount

To climb his happiness, would be well express'd

In our condition.

Poet

Nay, sir, but hear me on.

All those which were his fellows but of late,

Some better than his value, on the moment

Follow his strides, his lobbies fill with tendance,

Rain sacrificial whisperings in his ear,

Make sacred even his stirrup, and through him

Drink the free air.

Painter

Ay, marry, what of these?

Poet

When Fortune in her shift and change of mood

Spurns down her late beloved, all his dependants

Which labour'd after him to the mountain's top

Even on their knees and hands, let him slip down,

Not one accompanying his declining foot.

Painter

'Tis common:

A thousand moral paintings I can show

That shall demonstrate these quick blows of Fortune's

More pregnantly than words. Yet you do well

To show Lord Timon that mean eyes have seen

The foot above the head.

Trumpets sound.

*Enter TIMON, addressing himself courteously to every suitor; a Messenger from VENTIDIUS talking with him; LUCILIUS and other servants following*

TIMON

Imprison'd is he, say you?

Messenger

Ay, my good lord: five talents is his debt,

His means most short, his creditors most strait:

Your honourable letter he desires

To those have shut him up; which failing,

Periods his comfort.

TIMON

Noble Ventidius! Well;

I am not of that feather to shake off

My friend when he must need me. I do know him

A gentleman that well deserves a help:

Which he shall have: I'll pay the debt,

and free him.

Messenger

Your lordship ever binds him.

TIMON

Commend me to him: I will send his ransom;

And being enfranchised, bid him come to me.

'Tis not enough to help the feeble up,

But to support him after. Fare you well.

Messenger

All happiness to your honour!

*Exit*

*Enter an old Athenian*

Old Athenian

Lord Timon, hear me speak.

TIMON

Freely, good father.

Old Athenian

Thou hast a servant named Lucilius.

TIMON

I have so: what of him?

Old Athenian

Most noble Timon, call the man before thee.

TIMON

Attends he here, or no? Lucilius!

LUCILIUS

Here, at your lordship's service.

Old Athenian

This fellow here, Lord Timon, this thy creature,

By night frequents my house. I am a man

That from my first have been inclined to thrift;

And my estate deserves an heir more raised

Than one which holds a trencher.

TIMON

Well; what further?

Old Athenian

One only daughter have I, no kin else,

On whom I may confer what I have got:

The maid is fair, o' the youngest for a bride,

And I have bred her at my dearest cost

In qualities of the best. This man of thine

Attempts her love: I prithee, noble lord,

Join with me to forbid him her resort;

Myself have spoke in vain.

TIMON

The man is honest.

Old Athenian

Therefore he will be, Timon:

His honesty rewards him in itself;

It must not bear my daughter.

TIMON

Does she love him?

Old Athenian

She is young and apt:

Our own precedent passions do instruct us

What levity's in youth.

TIMON

[To LUCILIUS] Love you the maid?

LUCILIUS

Ay, my good lord, and she accepts of it.

Old Athenian

If in her marriage my consent be missing,

I call the gods to witness, I will choose

Mine heir from forth the beggars of the world,

And dispossess her all.

TIMON

How shall she be endow'd,

if she be mated with an equal husband?

Old Athenian

Three talents on the present; in future, all.

TIMON

This gentleman of mine hath served me long:

To build his fortune I will strain a little,

For 'tis a bond in men. Give him thy daughter:

What you bestow, in him I'll counterpoise,

And make him weigh with her.

Old Athenian

Most noble lord,

Pawn me to this your honour, she is his.

TIMON

My hand to thee; mine honour on my promise.

LUCILIUS

Humbly I thank your lordship: never may

The state or fortune fall into my keeping,

Which is not owed to you!

*Exeunt LUCILIUS and Old Athenian*

Poet

Vouchsafe my labour, and long live your lordship!

TIMON

I thank you; you shall hear from me anon:

Go not away. What have you there, my friend?

Painter

A piece of painting, which I do beseech

Your lordship to accept.

TIMON

Painting is welcome.

The painting is almost the natural man;

or since dishonour traffics with man's nature,

He is but outside: these pencill'd figures are

Even such as they give out. I like your work;

And you shall find I like it: wait attendance

Till you hear further from me.

Painter

The gods preserve ye!

TIMON

Well fare you, gentleman: give me your hand;

We must needs dine together. Sir, your jewel

Hath suffer'd under praise.

Jeweller

What, my lord! dispraise?

TIMON

A more satiety of commendations.

If I should pay you for't as 'tis extoll'd,

It would unclew me quite.

Jeweller

My lord, 'tis rated

As those which sell would give: but you well know,

Things of like value differing in the owners

Are prized by their masters: believe't, dear lord,

You mend the jewel by the wearing it.

TIMON

Well mock'd.

Merchant

No, my good lord; he speaks the common tongue,

Which all men speak with him.

TIMON

Look, who comes here: will you be chid?

*Enter APEMANTUS*

Jeweller: We'll bear, with your lordship.

Merchant

He'll spare none.

TIMON

Good morrow to thee, gentle Apemantus!

APEMANTUS

Till I be gentle, stay thou for thy good morrow;

When thou art Timon's dog, and these knaves honest.

TIMON

Why dost thou call them knaves? thou know'st them not.

APEMANTUS

Are they not Athenians?

TIMON

Yes.

APEMANTUS

Then I repent not.

Jeweller: You know me, Apemantus?

APEMANTUS

Thou know'st I do: I call'd thee by thy name.

TIMON

Thou art proud, Apemantus.

APEMANTUS

Of nothing so much as that I am not like Timon.

TIMON

Whither art going?

APEMANTUS

To knock out an honest Athenian's brains.

TIMON

That's a deed thou'lt die for.

APEMANTUS

Right, if doing nothing be death by the law.

TIMON

How likest thou this picture, Apemantus?

APEMANTUS

The best, for the innocence.

TIMON

Wrought he not well that painted it?

APEMANTUS

He wrought better that made the painter; and yet

he's but a filthy piece of work.

Painter

You're a dog.

APEMANTUS

Thy mother's of my generation: what's she, if I be a dog?

TIMON

Wilt dine with me, Apemantus?

APEMANTUS

No; I eat not lords.

TIMON

An thou shouldst, thou 'ldst anger ladies.

APEMANTUS

O, they eat lords; so they come by great bellies.

TIMON

That's a lascivious apprehension.

APEMANTUS

So thou apprehendest it: take it for thy labour.

TIMON

How dost thou like this jewel, Apemantus?

APEMANTUS

Not so well as plain-dealing, which will not cost a
man a doit.

TIMON

What dost thou think 'tis worth?

APEMANTUS

Not worth my thinking. How now, poet!

Poet

How now, philosopher!

APEMANTUS

Thou liest.

Poet

Art not one?

APEMANTUS

Yes.

Poet

Then I lie not.

APEMANTUS

Art not a poet?

Poet

Yes.

APEMANTUS

Then thou liest: look in thy last work, where thou

hast feigned him a worthy fellow.

Poet

That's not feigned; he is so.

APEMANTUS

Yes, he is worthy of thee, and to pay thee for thy

labour: he that loves to be flattered is worthy o'

the flatterer. Heavens, that I were a lord!

TIMON

What wouldst do then, Apemantus?

APEMANTUS

E'en as Apemantus does now; hate a lord with my heart.

TIMON

What, thyself?

APEMANTUS

Ay.

TIMON

Wherefore?

APEMANTUS

That I had no angry wit to be a lord.

Art not thou a merchant?

Merchant

Ay, Apemantus.

APEMANTUS

Traffic confound thee, if the gods will not!

Merchant

If traffic do it, the gods do it.

APEMANTUS

Traffic's thy god; and thy god confound thee!

Trumpet sounds.

*Enter a Messenger*

TIMON

What trumpet's that?

Messenger

'Tis Alcibiades, and some twenty horse,

All of companionship.

TIMON

Pray, entertain them; give them guide to us.

*Exeunt some Attendants*

You must needs dine with me: go not you hence

Till I have thank'd you: when dinner's done,

Show me this piece. I am joyful of your sights.

*Enter ALCIBIADES, with the rest*

Most welcome, sir!

APEMANTUS

So, so, there!

Aches contract and starve your supple joints!

That there should be small love 'mongst these

sweet knaves,

And all this courtesy! The strain of man's bred out

Into baboon and monkey.

ALCIBIADES

Sir, you have saved my longing, and I feed

Most hungerly on your sight.

TIMON

Right welcome, sir!

Ere we depart, we'll share a bounteous time

In different pleasures. Pray you, let us in.

    *Exeunt all except APEMANTUS*

    *Enter two Lords*

First Lord

What time o' day is't, Apemantus?

APEMANTUS

Time to be honest.

First Lord

That time serves still.

APEMANTUS

The more accursed thou, that still omitt'st it.

Second Lord

Thou art going to Lord Timon's feast?

APEMANTUS

Ay, to see meat fill knaves and wine heat fools.

Second Lord

Fare thee well, fare thee well.

APEMANTUS

Thou art a fool to bid me farewell twice.

Second Lord

Why, Apemantus?

APEMANTUS

Shouldst have kept one to thyself, for I mean to
give thee none.

First Lord

Hang thyself!

APEMANTUS

No, I will do nothing at thy bidding: make thy
requests to thy friend.

Second Lord

Away, unpeaceable dog, or I'll spurn thee hence!

APEMANTUS

I will fly, like a dog, the heels o' the ass.

*Exit*

First Lord

He's opposite to humanity. Come, shall we in,
And taste Lord Timon's bounty? he outgoes
The very heart of kindness.

Second Lord

He pours it out; Plutus, the god of gold,
Is but his steward: no meed, but he repays
Sevenfold above itself; no gift to him,
But breeds the giver a return exceeding

All use of quittance.

First Lord

The noblest mind he carries

That ever govern'd man.

Second Lord

Long may he live in fortunes! Shall we in?

First Lord

I'll keep you company.

*Exeunt*


## SCENE II. A banqueting-room in Timon's house.

Hautboys playing loud music. A great banquet served in; FLAVIUS and others attending; then enter TIMON, ALCIBIADES, Lords, Senators, and VENTIDIUS. Then comes, dropping, after all, APEMANTUS, discontentedly, like himself

VENTIDIUS

Most honour'd Timon,

It hath pleased the gods to remember my father's age,

And call him to long peace.

He is gone happy, and has left me rich:

Then, as in grateful virtue I am bound

To your free heart, I do return those talents,

Doubled with thanks and service, from whose help

I derived liberty.

TIMON

O, by no means,

Honest Ventidius; you mistake my love:

I gave it freely ever; and there's none

Can truly say he gives, if he receives:

If our betters play at that game, we must not dare

To imitate them; faults that are rich are fair.

VENTIDIUS

A noble spirit!

TIMON

Nay, my lords,

They all stand ceremoniously looking on TIMON

Ceremony was but devised at first

To set a gloss on faint deeds, hollow welcomes,

Recanting goodness, sorry ere 'tis shown;

But where there is true friendship, there needs none.

Pray, sit; more welcome are ye to my fortunes

Than my fortunes to me.

They sit

First Lord

My lord, we always have confess'd it.

APEMANTUS

Ho, ho, confess'd it! hang'd it, have you not?

TIMON

O, Apemantus, you are welcome.

APEMANTUS

No;

You shall not make me welcome:

I come to have thee thrust me out of doors.

TIMON

Fie, thou'rt a churl; ye've got a humour there

Does not become a man: 'tis much to blame.
They say, my lords, 'ira furor brevis est;' but yond
man is ever angry. Go, let him have a table by
himself, for he does neither affect company, nor is
he fit for't, indeed.

APEMANTUS

Let me stay at thine apperil, Timon: I come to
observe; I give thee warning on't.

TIMON

I take no heed of thee; thou'rt an Athenian,
therefore welcome: I myself would have no power;
prithee, let my meat make thee silent.

APEMANTUS

I scorn thy meat; 'twould choke me, for I should
ne'er flatter thee. O you gods, what a number of
men eat Timon, and he sees 'em not! It grieves me
to see so many dip their meat in one man's blood;
and all the madness is, he cheers them up too.
I wonder men dare trust themselves with men:
Methinks they should invite them without knives;
Good for their meat, and safer for their lives.
There's much example for't; the fellow that sits
next him now, parts bread with him, pledges the
breath of him in a divided draught, is the readiest
man to kill him: 't has been proved. If I were a
huge man, I should fear to drink at meals;
Lest they should spy my windpipe's dangerous notes:

Great men should drink with harness on their throats.

TIMON

My lord, in heart; and let the health go round.

Second Lord

Let it flow this way, my good lord.

APEMANTUS

Flow this way! A brave fellow! he keeps his tides

well. Those healths will make thee and thy state

look ill, Timon. Here's that which is too weak to

be a sinner, honest water, which ne'er left man i' the mire:

This and my food are equals; there's no odds:

Feasts are too proud to give thanks to the gods.

Apemantus' grace.

Immortal gods, I crave no pelf;

I pray for no man but myself:

Grant I may never prove so fond,

To trust man on his oath or bond;

Or a harlot, for her weeping;

Or a dog, that seems a-sleeping:

Or a keeper with my freedom;

Or my friends, if I should need 'em.

Amen. So fall to't:

Rich men sin, and I eat root.

Eats and drinks

Much good dich thy good heart, Apemantus!

TIMON

Captain Alcibiades, your heart's in the field now.

ALCIBIADES

My heart is ever at your service, my lord.

TIMON

You had rather be at a breakfast of enemies than a
dinner of friends.

ALCIBIADES

So the were bleeding-new, my lord, there's no meat
like 'em: I could wish my best friend at such a feast.

APEMANTUS

Would all those fatterers were thine enemies then,
that then thou mightst kill 'em and bid me to 'em!

First Lord

Might we but have that happiness, my lord, that you
would once use our hearts, whereby we might express
some part of our zeals, we should think ourselves
for ever perfect.

TIMON

O, no doubt, my good friends, but the gods
themselves have provided that I shall have much help
from you: how had you been my friends else? why
have you that charitable title from thousands, did
not you chiefly belong to my heart? I have told
more of you to myself than you can with modesty
speak in your own behalf; and thus far I confirm
you. O you gods, think I, what need we have any
friends, if we should ne'er have need of 'em? they
were the most needless creatures living, should we

ne'er have use for 'em, and would most resemble
sweet instruments hung up in cases that keep their
sounds to themselves. Why, I have often wished
myself poorer, that I might come nearer to you. We
are born to do benefits: and what better or
properer can we can our own than the riches of our
friends? O, what a precious comfort 'tis, to have
so many, like brothers, commanding one another's
fortunes! O joy, e'en made away ere 't can be born!
Mine eyes cannot hold out water, methinks: to
forget their faults, I drink to you.

APEMANTUS

Thou weepest to make them drink, Timon.

Second Lord

Joy had the like conception in our eyes
And at that instant like a babe sprung up.

APEMANTUS

Ho, ho! I laugh to think that babe a bastard.

Third Lord

I promise you, my lord, you moved me much.

APEMANTUS

Much!

Tucket, within

TIMON

What means that trump?

*Enter a Servant*

How now?

Servant

Please you, my lord, there are certain

ladies most desirous of admittance.

TIMON

Ladies! what are their wills?

Servant

There comes with them a forerunner, my lord, which

bears that office, to signify their pleasures.

TIMON

I pray, let them be admitted.

*Enter Cupid*

Cupid

Hail to thee, worthy Timon, and to all

That of his bounties taste! The five best senses

Acknowledge thee their patron; and come freely

To gratulate thy plenteous bosom: th' ear,

Taste, touch and smell, pleased from thy tale rise;

They only now come but to feast thine eyes.

TIMON

They're welcome all; let 'em have kind admittance:

Music, make their welcome!

*Exit Cupid*

First Lord

You see, my lord, how ample you're beloved.

Music.

*Re-enter Cupid with a mask of Ladies as Amazons, with lutes in their hands, dancing and playing*

APEMANTUS

Hoy-day, what a sweep of vanity comes this way!

They dance! they are mad women.

Like madness is the glory of this life.

As this pomp shows to a little oil and root.

We make ourselves fools, to disport ourselves;

And spend our flatteries, to drink those men

Upon whose age we void it up again,

With poisonous spite and envy.

Who lives that's not depraved or depraves?

Who dies, that bears not one spurn to their graves

Of their friends' gift?

I should fear those that dance before me now

Would one day stamp upon me: 't has been done;

Men shut their doors against a setting sun.

The Lords rise from table, with much adoring of TIMON; and to show their loves, each singles out an Amazon, and all dance, men with women, a lofty strain or two to the hautboys, and cease

TIMON

You have done our pleasures much grace, fair ladies,

Set a fair fashion on our entertainment,

Which was not half so beautiful and kind;

You have added worth unto 't and lustre,

And entertain'd me with mine own device;

I am to thank you for 't.

First Lady

My lord, you take us even at the best.

APEMANTUS

'Faith, for the worst is filthy; and would not hold

taking, I doubt me.

TIMON

Ladies, there is an idle banquet attends you:

Please you to dispose yourselves.

All Ladies

Most thankfully, my lord.

*Exeunt Cupid and Ladies*

TIMON

Flavius.

FLAVIUS

My lord?

TIMON

The little casket bring me hither.

FLAVIUS

Yes, my lord. More jewels yet!

There is no crossing him in 's humour;

Aside

Else I should tell him,--well, i' faith I should,

When all's spent, he 'ld be cross'd then, an he could.

'Tis pity bounty had not eyes behind,

That man might ne'er be wretched for his mind.

*Exit*

First Lord

Where be our men?

Servant

Here, my lord, in readiness.

Second Lord

Our horses!

*Re-enter FLAVIUS, with the casket*

TIMON

O my friends,

I have one word to say to you: look you, my good lord,

I must entreat you, honour me so much

As to advance this jewel; accept it and wear it,

Kind my lord.

First Lord

I am so far already in your gifts,--

All

So are we all.

*Enter a Servant*

Servant

My lord, there are certain nobles of the senate

Newly alighted, and come to visit you.

TIMON

They are fairly welcome.

FLAVIUS

I beseech your honour,

Vouchsafe me a word; it does concern you near.

TIMON

Near! why then, another time I'll hear thee:

I prithee, let's be provided to show them

entertainment.

FLAVIUS

[Aside] I scarce know how.

*Enter a Second Servant*

Second Servant

May it please your honour, Lord Lucius,

Out of his free love, hath presented to you

Four milk-white horses, trapp'd in silver.

TIMON

I shall accept them fairly; let the presents

Be worthily entertain'd.

*Enter a third Servant*

How now! what news?

Third Servant

Please you, my lord, that honourable

gentleman, Lord Lucullus, entreats your company

to-morrow to hunt with him, and has sent your honour

two brace of greyhounds.

TIMON

I'll hunt with him; and let them be received,

Not without fair reward.

FLAVIUS

[Aside] What will this come to?

He commands us to provide, and give great gifts,

And all out of an empty coffer:

Nor will he know his purse, or yield me this,

To show him what a beggar his heart is,

Being of no power to make his wishes good:

His promises fly so beyond his state

That what he speaks is all in debt; he owes

For every word: he is so kind that he now

Pays interest for 't; his land's put to their books.

Well, would I were gently put out of office

Before I were forced out!

Happier is he that has no friend to feed

Than such that do e'en enemies exceed.

I bleed inwardly for my lord.

*Exit*

TIMON

You do yourselves

Much wrong, you bate too much of your own merits:

Here, my lord, a trifle of our love.

Second Lord

With more than common thanks I will receive it.

Third Lord

O, he's the very soul of bounty!

TIMON

And now I remember, my lord, you gave

Good words the other day of a bay courser

I rode on: it is yours, because you liked it.

Second Lord

O, I beseech you, pardon me, my lord, in that.

TIMON

You may take my word, my lord; I know, no man

Can justly praise but what he does affect:

I weigh my friend's affection with mine own;

I'll tell you true. I'll call to you.

All Lords

O, none so welcome.

TIMON

I take all and your several visitations

So kind to heart, 'tis not enough to give;

Methinks, I could deal kingdoms to my friends,

And ne'er be weary. Alcibiades,

Thou art a soldier, therefore seldom rich;

It comes in charity to thee: for all thy living

Is 'mongst the dead, and all the lands thou hast

Lie in a pitch'd field.

ALCIBIADES

Ay, defiled land, my lord.

First Lord

We are so virtuously bound--

TIMON

And so

Am I to you.

Second Lord

So infinitely endear'd--

TIMON

All to you. Lights, more lights!

First Lord

The best of happiness,

Honour and fortunes, keep with you, Lord Timon!

TIMON

Ready for his friends.

*Exeunt all but APEMANTUS and TIMON*

**APEMANTUS**

What a coil's here!

Serving of becks and jutting-out of bums!

I doubt whether their legs be worth the sums

That are given for 'em. Friendship's full of dregs:

Methinks, false hearts should never have sound legs,

Thus honest fools lay out their wealth on court'sies.

**TIMON**

Now, Apemantus, if thou wert not sullen, I would be

good to thee.

**APEMANTUS**

No, I'll nothing: for if I should be bribed too,

there would be none left to rail upon thee, and then

thou wouldst sin the faster. Thou givest so long,

Timon, I fear me thou wilt give away thyself in

paper shortly: what need these feasts, pomps and

vain-glories?

**TIMON**

Nay, an you begin to rail on society once, I am

sworn not to give regard to you. Farewell; and come

with better music.

*Exit*

**APEMANTUS**

So:

Thou wilt not hear me now; thou shalt not then:

I'll lock thy heaven from thee.

O, that men's ears should be

To counsel deaf, but not to flattery!

*Exit*

# ACT II

## SCENE I. A Senator's house.

*Enter Senator, with papers in his hand*

Senator

And late, five thousand: to Varro and to Isidore

He owes nine thousand; besides my former sum,

Which makes it five and twenty. Still in motion

Of raging waste? It cannot hold; it will not.

If I want gold, steal but a beggar's dog,

And give it Timon, why, the dog coins gold.

If I would sell my horse, and buy twenty more

Better than he, why, give my horse to Timon,

Ask nothing, give it him, it foals me, straight,

And able horses. No porter at his gate,

But rather one that smiles and still invites

All that pass by. It cannot hold: no reason

Can found his state in safety. Caphis, ho!

Caphis, I say!

*Enter CAPHIS*

CAPHIS

Here, sir; what is your pleasure?

Senator

Get on your cloak, and haste you to Lord Timon;

Importune him for my moneys; be not ceased

With slight denial, nor then silenced when--

'Commend me to your master'--and the cap

Plays in the right hand, thus: but tell him,

My uses cry to me, I must serve my turn

Out of mine own; his days and times are past

And my reliances on his fracted dates

Have smit my credit: I love and honour him,

But must not break my back to heal his finger;

Immediate are my needs, and my relief

Must not be toss'd and turn'd to me in words,

But find supply immediate. Get you gone:

Put on a most importunate aspect,

A visage of demand; for, I do fear,

When every feather sticks in his own wing,

Lord Timon will be left a naked gull,

Which flashes now a phoenix. Get you gone.

CAPHIS

I go, sir.

Senator

'I go, sir!'--Take the bonds along with you,

And have the dates in contempt.

CAPHIS

I will, sir.

Senator

Go.

    *Exeunt*

## SCENE II. The same. A hall in Timon's house.

*Enter FLAVIUS, with many bills in his hand*

FLAVIUS

No care, no stop! so senseless of expense,

That he will neither know how to maintain it,

Nor cease his flow of riot: takes no account

How things go from him, nor resumes no care

Of what is to continue: never mind

Was to be so unwise, to be so kind.

What shall be done? he will not hear, till feel:

I must be round with him, now he comes from hunting.

Fie, fie, fie, fie!

*Enter CAPHIS, and the Servants of Isidore and Varro*

CAPHIS

Good even, Varro: what,

You come for money?

Varro's Servant Is't not your business too?

CAPHIS

It is: and yours too, Isidore?

Isidore's Servant It is so.

CAPHIS

Would we were all discharged!

Varro's Servant I fear it.

CAPHIS

Here comes the lord.

*Enter TIMON, ALCIBIADES, and Lords, & c*

TIMON

So soon as dinner's done, we'll forth again,

My Alcibiades. With me? what is your will?

CAPHIS

My lord, here is a note of certain dues.

TIMON

Dues! Whence are you?

CAPHIS

Of Athens here, my lord.

TIMON

Go to my steward.

CAPHIS

Please it your lordship, he hath put me off

To the succession of new days this month:

My master is awaked by great occasion

To call upon his own, and humbly prays you

That with your other noble parts you'll suit

In giving him his right.

TIMON

Mine honest friend,

I prithee, but repair to me next morning.

CAPHIS

Nay, good my lord,--

TIMON

Contain thyself, good friend.

Varro's Servant One Varro's servant, my good lord,--

Isidore's Servant From Isidore;

He humbly prays your speedy payment.

CAPHIS

If you did know, my lord, my master's wants--

Varro's Servant 'Twas due on forfeiture, my lord, six weeks And past.

Isidore's Servant Your steward puts me off, my lord;

And I am sent expressly to your lordship.

TIMON

Give me breath.

I do beseech you, good my lords, keep on;

I'll wait upon you instantly.

*Exeunt ALCIBIADES and Lords*

To FLAVIUS

Come hither: pray you,

How goes the world, that I am thus encounter'd

With clamourous demands of date-broke bonds,

And the detention of long-since-due debts,

Against my honour?

FLAVIUS

Please you, gentlemen,

The time is unagreeable to this business:

Your importunacy cease till after dinner,

That I may make his lordship understand

Wherefore you are not paid.

TIMON

Do so, my friends. See them well entertain'd.

*Exit*

FLAVIUS

Pray, draw near.

*Exit*

*Enter APEMANTUS and Fool*

CAPHIS

Stay, stay, here comes the fool with Apemantus:

let's ha' some sport with 'em.

Varro's Servant Hang him, he'll abuse us.

Isidore's Servant A plague upon him, dog!

Varro's Servant How dost, fool?

APEMANTUS

Dost dialogue with thy shadow?

Varro's Servant I speak not to thee.

APEMANTUS

No,'tis to thyself.

To the Fool

Come away.

Isidore's Servant There's the fool hangs on your back already.

APEMANTUS

No, thou stand'st single, thou'rt not on him yet.

CAPHIS

Where's the fool now?

APEMANTUS

He last asked the question. Poor rogues, and

usurers' men! bawds between gold and want!

All Servants

What are we, Apemantus?

APEMANTUS

Asses.

All Servants

Why?

APEMANTUS

That you ask me what you are, and do not know

yourselves. Speak to 'em, fool.

Fool

How do you, gentlemen?

All Servants

Gramercies, good fool: how does your mistress?

Fool

She's e'en setting on water to scald such chickens

as you are. Would we could see you at Corinth!

APEMANTUS

Good! gramercy.

*Enter Page*

Fool

Look you, here comes my mistress' page.

Page

[To the Fool] Why, how now, captain! what do you

in this wise company? How dost thou, Apemantus?

APEMANTUS

Would I had a rod in my mouth, that I might answer

thee profitably.

Page

Prithee, Apemantus, read me the superscription of

these letters: I know not which is which.

**APEMANTUS**

Canst not read?

Page

No.

**APEMANTUS**

There will little learning die then, that day thou

art hanged. This is to Lord Timon; this to

Alcibiades. Go; thou wast born a bastard, and thou't

die a bawd.

Page

Thou wast whelped a dog, and thou shalt famish a

dog's death. Answer not; I am gone.

*Exit*

**APEMANTUS**

E'en so thou outrunnest grace. Fool, I will go with

you to Lord Timon's.

Fool

Will you leave me there?

**APEMANTUS**

If Timon stay at home. You three serve three usurers?

All Servants

Ay; would they served us!

**APEMANTUS**

So would I,--as good a trick as ever hangman served thief.

Fool

Are you three usurers' men?

All Servants

Ay, fool.

Fool

I think no usurer but has a fool to his servant: my
mistress is one, and I am her fool. When men come
to borrow of your masters, they approach sadly, and
go away merry; but they enter my mistress' house
merrily, and go away sadly: the reason of this?

Varro's Servant I could render one.

APEMANTUS

Do it then, that we may account thee a whoremaster
and a knave; which not-withstanding, thou shalt be
no less esteemed.

Varro's Servant What is a whoremaster, fool?

Fool

A fool in good clothes, and something like thee.
'Tis a spirit: sometime't appears like a lord;
sometime like a lawyer; sometime like a philosopher,
with two stones moe than's artificial one: he is
very often like a knight; and, generally, in all
shapes that man goes up and down in from fourscore
to thirteen, this spirit walks in.

Varro's Servant Thou art not altogether a fool.

Fool

Nor thou altogether a wise man: as much foolery as
I have, so much wit thou lackest.

APEMANTUS

That answer might have become Apemantus.

All Servants

Aside, aside; here comes Lord Timon.

*Re-enter TIMON and FLAVIUS*

APEMANTUS

Come with me, fool, come.

Fool

I do not always follow lover, elder brother and
woman; sometime the philosopher.

*Exeunt APEMANTUS and Fool*

FLAVIUS

Pray you, walk near: I'll speak with you anon.

*Exeunt Servants*

TIMON

You make me marvel: wherefore ere this time

Had you not fully laid my state before me,

That I might so have rated my expense,

As I had leave of means?

FLAVIUS

You would not hear me,

At many leisures I proposed.

TIMON

Go to:

Perchance some single vantages you took.

When my indispos ition put you back:

And that unaptness made your minister,

Thus to excuse yourself.

FLAVIUS

O my good lord,

At many times I brought in my accounts,

Laid them before you; you would throw them off,

And say, you found them in mine honesty.

When, for some trifling present, you have bid me

Return so much, I have shook my head and wept;

Yea, 'gainst the authority of manners, pray'd you

To hold your hand more close: I did endure

Not seldom, nor no slight cheques, when I have

Prompted you in the ebb of your estate

And your great flow of debts. My loved lord,

Though you hear now, too late--yet now's a time--

The greatest of your having lacks a half

To pay your present debts.

TIMON

Let all my land be sold.

FLAVIUS

'Tis all engaged, some forfeited and gone;

And what remains will hardly stop the mouth

Of present dues: the future comes apace:

What shall defend the interim? and at length

How goes our reckoning?

TIMON

To Lacedaemon did my land extend.

FLAVIUS

O my good lord, the world is but a word:

Were it all yours to give it in a breath,

How quickly were it gone!

TIMON

You tell me true.

FLAVIUS

If you suspect my husbandry or falsehood,

Call me before the exactest auditors

And set me on the proof. So the gods bless me,

When all our offices have been oppress'd

With riotous feeders, when our vaults have wept

With drunken spilth of wine, when every room

Hath blazed with lights and bray'd with minstrelsy,

I have retired me to a wasteful cock,

And set mine eyes at flow.

TIMON

Prithee, no more.

FLAVIUS

Heavens, have I said, the bounty of this lord!

How many prodigal bits have slaves and peasants

This night englutted! Who is not Timon's?

What heart, head, sword, force, means, but is

Lord Timon's?

Great Timon, noble, worthy, royal Timon!

Ah, when the means are gone that buy this praise,

The breath is gone whereof this praise is made:

Feast-won, fast-lost; one cloud of winter showers,

These flies are couch'd.

TIMON

Come, sermon me no further:

No villanous bounty yet hath pass'd my heart;

Unwisely, not ignobly, have I given.

Why dost thou weep? Canst thou the conscience lack,

To think I shall lack friends? Secure thy heart;

If I would broach the vessels of my love,

And try the argument of hearts by borrowing,

Men and men's fortunes could I frankly use

As I can bid thee speak.

FLAVIUS

Assurance bless your thoughts!

TIMON

And, in some sort, these wants of mine are crown'd,

That I account them blessings; for by these

Shall I try friends: you shall perceive how you

Mistake my fortunes; I am wealthy in my friends.

Within there! Flaminius! Servilius!

*Enter FLAMINIUS, SERVILIUS, and other Servants*

Servants

My lord? my lord?

TIMON

I will dispatch you severally; you to Lord Lucius;

to Lord Lucullus you: I hunted with his honour

to-day: you, to Sempronius: commend me to their

loves, and, I am proud, say, that my occasions have

found time to use 'em toward a supply of money: let

the request be fifty talents.

FLAMINIUS

As you have said, my lord.

FLAVIUS

[Aside] Lord Lucius and Lucullus? hum!

TIMON

Go you, sir, to the senators--

Of whom, even to the state's best health, I have

Deserved this hearing--bid 'em send o' the instant

A thousand talents to me.

FLAVIUS

I have been bold--

For that I knew it the most general way--

To them to use your signet and your name;

But they do shake their heads, and I am here

No richer in return.

TIMON

Is't true? can't be?

FLAVIUS

They answer, in a joint and corporate voice,

That now they are at fall, want treasure, cannot

Do what they would; are sorry--you are honourable,--

But yet they could have wish'd--they know not--

Something hath been amiss--a noble nature

May catch a wrench--would all were well--'tis pity;--

And so, intending other serious matters,

After distasteful looks and these hard fractions,

With certain half-caps and cold-moving nods

They froze me into silence.

TIMON

You gods, reward them!

Prithee, man, look cheerly. These old fellows

Have their ingratitude in them hereditary:

Their blood is caked, 'tis cold, it seldom flows;

'Tis lack of kindly warmth they are not kind;

And nature, as it grows again toward earth,

Is fashion'd for the journey, dull and heavy.

To a Servant

Go to Ventidius.

To FLAVIUS

Prithee, be not sad,

Thou art true and honest; ingeniously I speak.

No blame belongs to thee.

To Servant

Ventidius lately

Buried his father; by whose death he's stepp'd

Into a great estate: when he was poor,

Imprison'd and in scarcity of friends,

I clear'd him with five talents: greet him from me;

Bid him suppose some good necessity

Touches his friend, which craves to be remember'd

With those five talents.

    *Exit Servant*

To FLAVIUS

That had, give't these fellows

To whom 'tis instant due. Ne'er speak, or think,

That Timon's fortunes 'mong his friends can sink.

FLAVIUS

I would I could not think it: that thought is

bounty's foe;

Being free itself, it thinks all others so.

*Exeunt*


# ACT III

## SCENE I. A room in Lucullus' house.

FLAMINIUS waiting.

*Enter a Servant to him*

Servant

I have told my lord of you; he is coming down to you.

FLAMINIUS

I thank you, sir.

*Enter LUCULLUS*

Servant

Here's my lord.

LUCULLUS

[Aside] One of Lord Timon's men? a gift, I

warrant. Why, this hits right; I dreamt of a silver

basin and ewer to-night. Flaminius, honest

Flaminius; you are very respectively welcome, sir.

Fill me some wine.

*Exit Servants*

And how does that honourable, complete, free-hearted

gentleman of Athens, thy very bountiful good lord
and master?

FLAMINIUS

His health is well sir.

LUCULLUS

I am right glad that his health is well, sir: and
what hast thou there under thy cloak, pretty Flaminius?

FLAMINIUS

'Faith, nothing but an empty box, sir; which, in my
lord's behalf, I come to entreat your honour to
supply; who, having great and instant occasion to
use fifty talents, hath sent to your lordship to
furnish him, nothing doubting your present
assistance therein.

LUCULLUS

La, la, la, la! 'nothing doubting,' says he? Alas,
good lord! a noble gentleman 'tis, if he would not
keep so good a house. Many a time and often I ha'
dined with him, and told him on't, and come again to
supper to him, of purpose to have him spend less,
and yet he would embrace no counsel, take no warning
by my coming. Every man has his fault, and honesty
is his: I ha' told him on't, but I could ne'er get
him from't.

*Re-enter Servant, with wine*

Servant

Please your lordship, here is the wine.

LUCULLUS

Flaminius, I have noted thee always wise. Here's to thee.

FLAMINIUS

Your lordship speaks your pleasure.

LUCULLUS

I have observed thee always for a towardly prompt

spirit--give thee thy due--and one that knows what

belongs to reason; and canst use the time well, if

the time use thee well: good parts in thee.

To Servant

Get you gone, sirrah.

*Exit Servant*

Draw nearer, honest Flaminius. Thy lord's a

bountiful gentleman: but thou art wise; and thou

knowest well enough, although thou comest to me,

that this is no time to lend money, especially upon

bare friendship, without security. Here's three

solidares for thee: good boy, wink at me, and say

thou sawest me not. Fare thee well.

FLAMINIUS

Is't possible the world should so much differ,

And we alive that lived? Fly, damned baseness,

To him that worships thee!

Throwing the money back

LUCULLUS

Ha! now I see thou art a fool, and fit for thy master.

*Exit*

FLAMINIUS

May these add to the number that may scald thee!

Let moulten coin be thy damnation,

Thou disease of a friend, and not himself!

Has friendship such a faint and milky heart,

It turns in less than two nights? O you gods,

I feel master's passion! this slave,

Unto his honour, has my lord's meat in him:

Why should it thrive and turn to nutriment,

When he is turn'd to poison?

O, may diseases only work upon't!

And, when he's sick to death, let not that part of nature

Which my lord paid for, be of any power

To expel sickness, but prolong his hour!

    *Exit*


## SCENE II. A public place.

    *Enter LUCILIUS, with three Strangers*

LUCILIUS

Who, the Lord Timon? he is my very good friend, and

an honourable gentleman.

First Stranger

We know him for no less, though we are but strangers

to him. But I can tell you one thing, my lord, and

which I hear from common rumours: now Lord Timon's

happy hours are done and past, and his estate

shrinks from him.

LUCILIUS

Fie, no, do not believe it; he cannot want for money.

Second Stranger

But believe you this, my lord, that, not long ago,

one of his men was with the Lord Lucullus to borrow

so many talents, nay, urged extremely for't and

showed what necessity belonged to't, and yet was denied.

LUCILIUS

How!

Second Stranger

I tell you, denied, my lord.

LUCILIUS

What a strange case was that! now, before the gods,

I am ashamed on't. Denied that honourable man!

there was very little honour showed in't. For my own

part, I must needs confess, I have received some

small kindnesses from him, as money, plate, jewels

and such-like trifles, nothing comparing to his;

yet, had he mistook him and sent to me, I should

ne'er have denied his occasion so many talents.

*Enter SERVILIUS*

SERVILIUS

See, by good hap, yonder's my lord;

I have sweat to see his honour. My honoured lord,--

To LUCIUS

LUCILIUS

Servilius! you are kindly met, sir. Fare thee well:

commend me to thy honourable virtuous lord, my very
exquisite friend.

SERVILIUS

May it please your honour, my lord hath sent--

LUCILIUS

Ha! what has he sent? I am so much endeared to
that lord; he's ever sending: how shall I thank
him, thinkest thou? And what has he sent now?

SERVILIUS

Has only sent his present occasion now, my lord;
requesting your lordship to supply his instant use
with so many talents.

LUCILIUS

I know his lordship is but merry with me;
He cannot want fifty five hundred talents.

SERVILIUS

But in the mean time he wants less, my lord.
If his occasion were not virtuous,
I should not urge it half so faithfully.

LUCILIUS

Dost thou speak seriously, Servilius?

SERVILIUS

Upon my soul,'tis true, sir.

LUCILIUS

What a wicked beast was I to disfurnish myself
against such a good time, when I might ha' shown
myself honourable! how unluckily it happened, that I

should purchase the day before for a little part,

and undo a great deal of honoured! Servilius, now,

before the gods, I am not able to do,--the more

beast, I say:--I was sending to use Lord Timon

myself, these gentlemen can witness! but I would

not, for the wealth of Athens, I had done't now.

Commend me bountifully to his good lordship; and I

hope his honour will conceive the fairest of me,

because I have no power to be kind: and tell him

this from me, I count it one of my greatest

afflictions, say, that I cannot pleasure such an

honourable gentleman. Good Servilius, will you

befriend me so far, as to use mine own words to him?

SERVILIUS

Yes, sir, I shall.

LUCILIUS

I'll look you out a good turn, Servilius.

*Exit SERVILIUS*

True as you said, Timon is shrunk indeed;

And he that's once denied will hardly speed.

*Exit*

First Stranger

Do you observe this, Hostilius?

Second Stranger

Ay, too well.

First Stranger

Why, this is the world's soul; and just of the

same piece

Is every flatterer's spirit. Who can call him

His friend that dips in the same dish? for, in

My knowing, Timon has been this lord's father,

And kept his credit with his purse,

Supported his estate; nay, Timon's money

Has paid his men their wages: he ne'er drinks,

But Timon's silver treads upon his lip;

And yet--O, see the monstrousness of man

When he looks out in an ungrateful shape!--

He does deny him, in respect of his,

What charitable men afford to beggars.

Third Stranger

Religion groans at it.

First Stranger

For mine own part,

I never tasted Timon in my life,

Nor came any of his bounties over me,

To mark me for his friend; yet, I protest,

For his right noble mind, illustrious virtue

And honourable carriage,

Had his necessity made use of me,

I would have put my wealth into donation,

And the best half should have return'd to him,

So much I love his heart: but, I perceive,

Men must learn now with pity to dispense;

For policy sits above conscience.

## SCENE III. A room in Sempronius' house.

*Enter SEMPRONIUS, and a Servant of TIMON's*

SEMPRONIUS

Must he needs trouble me in 't,--hum!--'bove

all others?

He might have tried Lord Lucius or Lucullus;

And now Ventidius is wealthy too,

Whom he redeem'd from prison: all these

Owe their estates unto him.

Servant

My lord,

They have all been touch'd and found base metal, for

They have au denied him.

SEMPRONIUS

How! have they denied him?

Has Ventidius and Lucullus denied him?

And does he send to me? Three? hum!

It shows but little love or judgment in him:

Must I be his last refuge! His friends, like

physicians,

Thrive, give him over: must I take the cure upon me?

Has much disgraced me in't; I'm angry at him,

That might have known my place: I see no sense for't,

But his occasion might have woo'd me first;

For, in my conscience, I was the first man

That e'er received gift from him:

And does he think so backwardly of me now,

That I'll requite its last? No:

So it may prove an argument of laughter

To the rest, and 'mongst lords I be thought a fool.

I'ld rather than the worth of thrice the sum,

Had sent to me first, but for my mind's sake;

I'd such a courage to do him good. But now return,

And with their faint reply this answer join;

Who bates mine honour shall not know my coin.

*Exit*

Servant

Excellent! Your lordship's a goodly villain. The

devil knew not what he did when he made man

politic; he crossed himself by 't: and I cannot

think but, in the end, the villainies of man will

set him clear. How fairly this lord strives to

appear foul! takes virtuous copies to be wicked,

like those that under hot ardent zeal would set

whole realms on fire: Of such a nature is his

politic love.

This was my lord's best hope; now all are fled,

Save only the gods: now his friends are dead,

Doors, that were ne'er acquainted with their wards

Many a bounteous year must be employ'd

Now to guard sure their master.

And this is all a liberal course allows;

Who cannot keep his wealth must keep his house.

*Exit*


## SCENE IV. The same. A hall in Timon's house.

*Enter two Servants of Varro, and the Servant of LUCIUS, meeting TITUS, HORTENSIUS, and other Servants of TIMON's creditors, waiting his coming out*

Varro's

First Servant

Well met; good morrow, Titus and Hortensius.

TITUS

The like to you kind Varro.

HORTENSIUS

Lucius!

What, do we meet together?

Lucilius' Servant Ay, and I think

One business does command us all; for mine Is money.

TITUS

So is theirs and ours.

*Enter PHILOTUS*

Lucilius' Servant And Sir Philotus too!

PHILOTUS

Good day at once.

Lucilius' Servant Welcome, good brother.

What do you think the hour?

PHILOTUS

Labouring for nine.

Lucilius' Servant So much?

PHILOTUS

Is not my lord seen yet?

Lucilius' Servant Not yet.

PHILOTUS

I wonder on't; he was wont to shine at seven.

Lucilius' Servant Ay, but the days are wax'd shorter with him:

You must consider that a prodigal course

Is like the sun's; but not, like his, recoverable.

I fear 'tis deepest winter in Lord Timon's purse;

That is one may reach deep enough, and yet

Find little.

PHILOTUS

I am of your fear for that.

TITUS

I'll show you how to observe a strange event.

Your lord sends now for money.

HORTENSIUS

Most true, he does.

TITUS

And he wears jewels now of Timon's gift,

For which I wait for money.

HORTENSIUS

It is against my heart.

Lucilius' Servant Mark, how strange it shows,

Timon in this should pay more than he owes:

And e'en as if your lord should wear rich jewels,

And send for money for 'em.

HORTENSIUS

I'm weary of this charge, the gods can witness:

I know my lord hath spent of Timon's wealth,

And now ingratitude makes it worse than stealth.

Varro's

First Servant

Yes, mine's three thousand crowns: what's yours?

Lucilius' Servant Five thousand mine.

Varro's

First Servant

'Tis much deep: and it should seem by the sum,

Your master's confidence was above mine;

Else, surely, his had equall'd.

> *Enter FLAMINIUS.*

TITUS

One of Lord Timon's men.

Lucilius' Servant Flaminius! Sir, a word: pray, is my lord ready to

come forth?

FLAMINIUS

No, indeed, he is not.

TITUS

We attend his lordship; pray, signify so much.

FLAMINIUS

I need not tell him that; he knows you are too diligent.

> *Exit*

> *Enter FLAVIUS in a cloak, muffled*

Lucilius' Servant Ha! is not that his steward muffled so?

He goes away in a cloud: call him, call him.

TITUS

Do you hear, sir?

Varro's

Second Servant

By your leave, sir,--

FLAVIUS

What do ye ask of me, my friend?

TITUS

We wait for certain money here, sir.

FLAVIUS

Ay,

If money were as certain as your waiting,

'Twere sure enough.

Why then preferr'd you not your sums and bills,

When your false masters eat of my lord's meat?

Then they could smile and fawn upon his debts

And take down the interest into their

gluttonous maws.

You do yourselves but wrong to stir me up;

Let me pass quietly:

Believe 't, my lord and I have made an end;

I have no more to reckon, he to spend.

Lucilius' Servant Ay, but this answer will not serve.

FLAVIUS

If 'twill not serve,'tis not so base as you;

For you serve knaves.

*Exit*

Varro's

First Servant

How! what does his cashiered worship mutter?

Varro's

Second Servant

No matter what; he's poor, and that's revenge

enough. Who can speak broader than he that has no

house to put his head in? such may rail against

great buildings.

*Enter SERVILIUS*

TITUS

O, here's Servilius; now we shall know some answer.

SERVILIUS

If I might beseech you, gentlemen, to repair some

other hour, I should derive much from't; for,

take't of my soul, my lord leans wondrously to

discontent: his comfortable temper has forsook him;

he's much out of health, and keeps his chamber.

Lucilius' Servant: Many do keep their chambers are not sick:

And, if it be so far beyond his health,

Methinks he should the sooner pay his debts,

And make a clear way to the gods.

SERVILIUS

Good gods!

TITUS

We cannot take this for answer, sir.

FLAMINIUS

[Within] Servilius, help! My lord! my lord!

*Enter TIMON, in a rage, FLAMINIUS following*

TIMON

What, are my doors opposed against my passage?

Have I been ever free, and must my house

Be my retentive enemy, my gaol?

The place which I have feasted, does it now,

Like all mankind, show me an iron heart?

Lucilius' Servant Put in now, Titus.

TITUS

My lord, here is my bill.

Lucilius' Servant Here's mine.

HORTENSIUS

And mine, my lord.

Both

Varro's Servants And ours, my lord.

PHILOTUS

All our bills.

TIMON

Knock me down with 'em: cleave me to the girdle.

Lucilius' Servant Alas, my lord,-

TIMON

Cut my heart in sums.

TITUS

Mine, fifty talents.

TIMON

Tell out my blood.

Lucilius' Servant Five thousand crowns, my lord.

TIMON

Five thousand drops pays that.

What yours?--and yours?

Varro's

First Servant

My lord,--

Varro's

Second Servant

My lord,--

TIMON

Tear me, take me, and the gods fall upon you!

*Exit*

HORTENSIUS

'Faith, I perceive our masters may throw their caps

at their money: these debts may well be called

desperate ones, for a madman owes 'em.

*Exeunt*

*Re-enter TIMON and FLAVIUS*

TIMON

They have e'en put my breath from me, the slaves.

Creditors? devils!

FLAVIUS

My dear lord,--

TIMON

What if it should be so?

FLAVIUS

My lord,--

TIMON

I'll have it so. My steward!

FLAVIUS

Here, my lord.

TIMON

So fitly? Go, bid all my friends again,

Lucius, Lucullus, and Sempronius:

All, sirrah, all:

I'll once more feast the rascals.

FLAVIUS

O my lord,

You only speak from your distracted soul;

There is not so much left, to furnish out

A moderate table.

TIMON

Be't not in thy care; go,

I charge thee, invite them all: let in the tide

Of knaves once more; my cook and I'll provide.

*Exeunt*


## SCENE V. The same. The senate-house. The Senate sitting.

First Senator

My lord, you have my voice to it; the fault's

Bloody; 'tis necessary he should die:

Nothing emboldens sin so much as mercy.

**Second Senator**

Most true; the law shall bruise him.

*Enter ALCIBIADES, with Attendants*

**ALCIBIADES**

Honour, health, and compassion to the senate!

**First Senator**

Now, captain?

**ALCIBIADES**

I am an humble suitor to your virtues;

For pity is the virtue of the law,

And none but tyrants use it cruelly.

It pleases time and fortune to lie heavy

Upon a friend of mine, who, in hot blood,

Hath stepp'd into the law, which is past depth

To those that, without heed, do plunge into 't.

He is a man, setting his fate aside,

Of comely virtues:

Nor did he soil the fact with cowardice--

An honour in him which buys out his fault--

But with a noble fury and fair spirit,

Seeing his reputation touch'd to death,

He did oppose his foe:

And with such sober and unnoted passion

He did behave his anger, ere 'twas spent,

As if he had but proved an argument.

**First Senator**

You undergo too strict a paradox,

Striving to make an ugly deed look fair:

Your words have took such pains as if they labour'd

To bring manslaughter into form and set quarrelling

Upon the head of valour; which indeed

Is valour misbegot and came into the world

When sects and factions were newly born:

He's truly valiant that can wisely suffer

The worst that man can breathe, and make his wrongs

His outsides, to wear them like his raiment,

carelessly,

And ne'er prefer his injuries to his heart,

To bring it into danger.

If wrongs be evils and enforce us kill,

What folly 'tis to hazard life for ill!

ALCIBIADES

My lord,--

First Senator

You cannot make gross sins look clear:

To revenge is no valour, but to bear.

ALCIBIADES

My lords, then, under favour, pardon me,

If I speak like a captain.

Why do fond men expose themselves to battle,

And not endure all threats? sleep upon't,

And let the foes quietly cut their throats,

Without repugnancy? If there be

Such valour in the bearing, what make we

Abroad? why then, women are more valiant

That stay at home, if bearing carry it,

And the ass more captain than the lion, the felon

Loaden with irons wiser than the judge,

If wisdom be in suffering. O my lords,

As you are great, be pitifully good:

Who cannot condemn rashness in cold blood?

To kill, I grant, is sin's extremest gust;

But, in defence, by mercy, 'tis most just.

To be in anger is impiety;

But who is man that is not angry?

Weigh but the crime with this.

Second Senator

You breathe in vain.

ALCIBIADES

In vain! his service done

At Lacedaemon and Byzantium

Were a sufficient briber for his life.

First Senator

What's that?

ALCIBIADES

I say, my lords, he has done fair service,

And slain in fight many of your enemies:

How full of valour did he bear himself

In the last conflict, and made plenteous wounds!

Second Senator

He has made too much plenty with 'em;

He's a sworn rioter: he has a sin that often

Drowns him, and takes his valour prisoner:

If there were no foes, that were enough

To overcome him: in that beastly fury

He has been known to commit outrages,

And cherish factions: 'tis inferr'd to us,

His days are foul and his drink dangerous.

First Senator

He dies.

ALCIBIADES

Hard fate! he might have died in war.

My lords, if not for any parts in him--

Though his right arm might purchase his own time

And be in debt to none--yet, more to move you,

Take my deserts to his, and join 'em both:

And, for I know your reverend ages love

Security, I'll pawn my victories, all

My honours to you, upon his good returns.

If by this crime he owes the law his life,

Why, let the war receive 't in valiant gore

For law is strict, and war is nothing more.

First Senator

We are for law: he dies; urge it no more,

On height of our displeasure: friend or brother,

He forfeits his own blood that spills another.

ALCIBIADES

Must it be so? it must not be. My lords,

I do beseech you, know me.

Second Senator

How!

ALCIBIADES

Call me to your remembrances.

Third Senator

What!

ALCIBIADES

I cannot think but your age has forgot me;

It could not else be, I should prove so base,

To sue, and be denied such common grace:

My wounds ache at you.

First Senator

Do you dare our anger?

'Tis in few words, but spacious in effect;

We banish thee for ever.

ALCIBIADES

Banish me!

Banish your dotage; banish usury,

That makes the senate ugly.

First Senator

If, after two days' shine, Athens contain thee,

Attend our weightier judgment. And, not to swell

our spirit,

He shall be executed presently.

*Exeunt Senators*

ALCIBIADES

Now the gods keep you old enough; that you may live

Only in bone, that none may look on you!

I'm worse than mad: I have kept back their foes,

While they have told their money and let out

Their coin upon large interest, I myself

Rich only in large hurts. All those for this?

Is this the balsam that the usuring senate

Pours into captains' wounds? Banishment!

It comes not ill; I hate not to be banish'd;

It is a cause worthy my spleen and fury,

That I may strike at Athens. I'll cheer up

My discontented troops, and lay for hearts.

'Tis honour with most lands to be at odds;

Soldiers should brook as little wrongs as gods.

 *Exit*


## SCENE VI. The same. A banqueting-room in Timon's house.

Music. Tables set out: Servants attending.

 *Enter divers Lords, Senators and others, at several doors*

First Lord

The good time of day to you, sir.

Second Lord

I also wish it to you. I think this honourable lord

did but try us this other day.

First Lord

Upon that were my thoughts tiring, when we

encountered: I hope it is not so low with him as

he made it seem in the trial of his several friends.

Second Lord

It should not be, by the persuasion of his new feasting.

First Lord

I should think so: he hath sent me an earnest

inviting, which many my near occasions did urge me

to put off; but he hath conjured me beyond them, and

I must needs appear.

Second Lord

In like manner was I in debt to my importunate

business, but he would not hear my excuse. I am

sorry, when he sent to borrow of me, that my

provision was out.

First Lord

I am sick of that grief too, as I understand how all

things go.

Second Lord

Every man here's so. What would he have borrowed of

you?

First Lord

A thousand pieces.

Second Lord

A thousand pieces!

First Lord

What of you?

Second Lord

He sent to me, sir,--Here he comes.

*Enter TIMON and Attendants*

TIMON

With all my heart, gentlemen both; and how fare you?

First Lord

Ever at the best, hearing well of your lordship.

Second Lord

The swallow follows not summer more willing than we

your lordship.

TIMON

[Aside] Nor more willingly leaves winter; such

summer-birds are men. Gentlemen, our dinner will not

recompense this long stay: feast your ears with the

music awhile, if they will fare so harshly o' the

trumpet's sound; we shall to 't presently.

First Lord

I hope it remains not unkindly with your lordship

that I returned you an empty messenger.

TIMON

O, sir, let it not trouble you.

Second Lord

My noble lord,--

TIMON

Ah, my good friend, what cheer?

Second Lord

My most honourable lord, I am e'en sick of shame,

that, when your lordship this other day sent to me,

I was so unfortunate a beggar.

TIMON

Think not on 't, sir.

Second Lord

If you had sent but two hours before,--

TIMON

Let it not cumber your better remembrance.

The banquet brought in

Come, bring in all together.

Second Lord

All covered dishes!

First Lord

Royal cheer, I warrant you.

Third Lord

Doubt not that, if money and the season can yield

it.

First Lord

How do you? What's the news?

Third Lord

Alcibiades is banished: hear you of it?

First LordSecond Lord

Alcibiades banished!

Third Lord

'Tis so, be sure of it.

First Lord

How! how!

Second Lord

I pray you, upon what?

TIMON

My worthy friends, will you draw near?

Third Lord

I'll tell you more anon. Here's a noble feast toward.

Second Lord

This is the old man still.

Third Lord

Will 't hold? will 't hold?

Second Lord

It does: but time will--and so--

Third Lord

I do conceive.

TIMON

Each man to his stool, with that spur as he would to

the lip of his mistress: your diet shall be in all

places alike. Make not a city feast of it, to let

the meat cool ere we can agree upon the first place:

sit, sit. The gods require our thanks.

You great benefactors, sprinkle our society with

thankfulness. For your own gifts, make yourselves

praised: but reserve still to give, lest your

deities be despised. Lend to each man enough, that

one need not lend to another; for, were your

godheads to borrow of men, men would forsake the

gods. Make the meat be beloved more than the man

that gives it. Let no assembly of twenty be without

a score of villains: if there sit twelve women at

the table, let a dozen of them be--as they are. The

rest of your fees, O gods--the senators of Athens,

together with the common lag of people--what is

amiss in them, you gods, make suitable for

destruction. For these my present friends, as they

are to me nothing, so in nothing bless them, and to

nothing are they welcome.

Uncover, dogs, and lap.

The dishes are uncovered and seen to be full of warm water

Some Speak

What does his lordship mean?

Some Others

I know not.

TIMON

May you a better feast never behold,

You knot of mouth-friends I smoke and lukewarm water

Is your perfection. This is Timon's last;

Who, stuck and spangled with your flatteries,

Washes it off, and sprinkles in your faces

Your reeking villany.

Throwing the water in their faces

Live loathed and long,

Most smiling, smooth, detested parasites,

Courteous destroyers, affable wolves, meek bears,

You fools of fortune, trencher-friends, time's flies,

Cap and knee slaves, vapours, and minute-jacks!

Of man and beast the infinite malady

Crust you quite o'er! What, dost thou go?

Soft! take thy physic first--thou too--and thou;--

Stay, I will lend thee money, borrow none.

Throws the dishes at them, and drives them out

What, all in motion? Henceforth be no feast,

Whereat a villain's not a welcome guest.

Burn, house! sink, Athens! henceforth hated be

Of Timon man and all humanity!

*Exit*

*Re-enter the Lords, Senators, & c*

First Lord

How now, my lords!

Second Lord

Know you the quality of Lord Timon's fury?

Third Lord

Push! did you see my cap?

Fourth Lord

I have lost my gown.

First Lord

He's but a mad lord, and nought but humour sways him.

He gave me a jewel th' other day, and now he has

beat it out of my hat: did you see my jewel?

Third Lord

Did you see my cap?

Second Lord

Here 'tis.

Fourth Lord

Here lies my gown.

First Lord

Let's make no stay.

Second Lord

Lord Timon's mad.

Third Lord

I feel 't upon my bones.

Fourth Lord

One day he gives us diamonds, next day stones.

*Exeunt*

# ACT IV

## SCENE I. Without the walls of Athens.

*Enter TIMON*

TIMON

Let me look back upon thee. O thou wall,

That girdlest in those wolves, dive in the earth,

And fence not Athens! Matrons, turn incontinent!

Obedience fail in children! slaves and fools,

Pluck the grave wrinkled senate from the bench,

And minister in their steads! to general filths

Convert o' the instant, green virginity,

Do 't in your parents' eyes! bankrupts, hold fast;

Rather than render back, out with your knives,

And cut your trusters' throats! bound servants, steal!

Large-handed robbers your grave masters are,

And pill by law. Maid, to thy master's bed;

Thy mistress is o' the brothel! Son of sixteen,

pluck the lined crutch from thy old limping sire,

With it beat out his brains! Piety, and fear,

Religion to the gods, peace, justice, truth,

Domestic awe, night-rest, and neighbourhood,

Instruction, manners, mysteries, and trades,

Degrees, observances, customs, and laws,

Decline to your confounding contraries,

And let confusion live! Plagues, incident to men,

Your potent and infectious fevers heap

On Athens, ripe for stroke! Thou cold sciatica,

Cripple our senators, that their limbs may halt

As lamely as their manners. Lust and liberty

Creep in the minds and marrows of our youth,

That 'gainst the stream of virtue they may strive,

And drown themselves in riot! Itches, blains,

Sow all the Athenian bosoms; and their crop

Be general leprosy! Breath infect breath,

at their society, as their friendship, may

merely poison! Nothing I'll bear from thee,

But nakedness, thou detestable town!

Take thou that too, with multiplying bans!

Timon will to the woods; where he shall find

The unkindest beast more kinder than mankind.

The gods confound--hear me, you good gods all--

The Athenians both within and out that wall!

And grant, as Timon grows, his hate may grow

To the whole race of mankind, high and low! Amen.

*Exit*


## SCENE II. Athens. A room in Timon's house.

*Enter FLAVIUS, with two or three Servants*

First Servant

Hear you, master steward, where's our master?

Are we undone? cast off? nothing remaining?

FLAVIUS

Alack, my fellows, what should I say to you?

Let me be recorded by the righteous gods,

I am as poor as you.

First Servant

Such a house broke!

So noble a master fall'n! All gone! and not

One friend to take his fortune by the arm,

And go along with him!

Second Servant

As we do turn our backs

From our companion thrown into his grave,

So his familiars to his buried fortunes

Slink all away, leave their false vows with him,

Like empty purses pick'd; and his poor self,

A dedicated beggar to the air,

With his disease of all-shunn'd poverty,

Walks, like contempt, alone. More of our fellows.

*Enter other Servants*

FLAVIUS

All broken implements of a ruin'd house.

Third Servant

Yet do our hearts wear Timon's livery;

That see I by our faces; we are fellows still,

Serving alike in sorrow: leak'd is our bark,

And we, poor mates, stand on the dying deck,

Hearing the surges threat: we must all part

Into this sea of air.

FLAVIUS

Good fellows all,

The latest of my wealth I'll share amongst you.

Wherever we shall meet, for Timon's sake,

Let's yet be fellows; let's shake our heads, and say,

As 'twere a knell unto our master's fortunes,

'We have seen better days.' Let each take some;

Nay, put out all your hands. Not one word more:

Thus part we rich in sorrow, parting poor.

Servants embrace, and part several ways

O, the fierce wretchedness that glory brings us!

Who would not wish to be from wealth exempt,

Since riches point to misery and contempt?

Who would be so mock'd with glory? or to live

But in a dream of friendship?

To have his pomp and all what state compounds

But only painted, like his varnish'd friends?

Poor honest lord, brought low by his own heart,

Undone by goodness! Strange, unusual blood,

When man's worst sin is, he does too much good!

Who, then, dares to be half so kind again?

For bounty, that makes gods, does still mar men.

My dearest lord, bless'd, to be most accursed,

Rich, only to be wretched, thy great fortunes

Are made thy chief afflictions. Alas, kind lord!

He's flung in rage from this ingrateful seat

Of monstrous friends, nor has he with him to

Supply his life, or that which can command it.

I'll follow and inquire him out:

I'll ever serve his mind with my best will;

Whilst I have gold, I'll be his steward still.

    *Exit*


## SCENE III. Woods and cave, near the seashore.

*Enter TIMON, from the cave*

O blessed breeding sun, draw from the earth

Rotten humidity; below thy sister's orb

Infect the air! Twinn'd brothers of one womb,

Whose procreation, residence, and birth,

Scarce is dividant, touch them with several fortunes;

The greater scorns the lesser: not nature,

To whom all sores lay siege, can bear great fortune,

But by contempt of nature.

Raise me this beggar, and deny 't that lord;

The senator shall bear contempt hereditary,

The beggar native honour.

It is the pasture lards the rother's sides,

The want that makes him lean. Who dares, who dares,

In purity of manhood stand upright,

And say 'This man's a flatterer?' if one be,

So are they all; for every grise of fortune

Is smooth'd by that below: the learned pate

Ducks to the golden fool: all is oblique;

There's nothing level in our cursed natures,

But direct villany. Therefore, be abhorr'd

All feasts, societies, and throngs of men!

His semblable, yea, himself, Timon disdains:

Destruction fang mankind! Earth, yield me roots!

Digging

Who seeks for better of thee, sauce his palate

With thy most operant poison! What is here?

Gold? yellow, glittering, precious gold? No, gods,

I am no idle votarist: roots, you clear heavens!

Thus much of this will make black white, foul fair,

Wrong right, base noble, old young, coward valiant.

Ha, you gods! why this? what this, you gods? Why, this

Will lug your priests and servants from your sides,

Pluck stout men's pillows from below their heads:

This yellow slave

Will knit and break religions, bless the accursed,

Make the hoar leprosy adored, place thieves

And give them title, knee and approbation

With senators on the bench: this is it

That makes the wappen'd widow wed again;

She, whom the spital-house and ulcerous sores

Would cast the gorge at, this embalms and spices

To the April day again. Come, damned earth,

Thou common whore of mankind, that put'st odds

Among the route of nations, I will make thee

Do thy right nature.

March afar off

Ha! a drum ? Thou'rt quick,

But yet I'll bury thee: thou'lt go, strong thief,

When gouty keepers of thee cannot stand.

Nay, stay thou out for earnest.

Keeping some gold

> *Enter ALCIBIADES, with drum and fife, in warlike manner; PHRYNIA and TIMANDRA*

ALCIBIADES

What art thou there? speak.

TIMON

A beast, as thou art. The canker gnaw thy heart,

For showing me again the eyes of man!

ALCIBIADES

What is thy name? Is man so hateful to thee,

That art thyself a man?

TIMON

I am Misanthropos, and hate mankind.

For thy part, I do wish thou wert a dog,

That I might love thee something.

ALCIBIADES

I know thee well;

But in thy fortunes am unlearn'd and strange.

TIMON

I know thee too; and more than that I know thee,

I not desire to know. Follow thy drum;

With man's blood paint the ground, gules, gules:

Religious canons, civil laws are cruel;

Then what should war be? This fell whore of thine

Hath in her more destruction than thy sword,

For all her cherubim look.

PHRYNIA

Thy lips rot off!

TIMON

I will not kiss thee; then the rot returns

To thine own lips again.

ALCIBIADES

How came the noble Timon to this change?

TIMON

As the moon does, by wanting light to give:

But then renew I could not, like the moon;

There were no suns to borrow of.

ALCIBIADES

Noble Timon,

What friendship may I do thee?

TIMON

None, but to

Maintain my opinion.

ALCIBIADES

What is it, Timon?

TIMON

Promise me friendship, but perform none: if thou

wilt not promise, the gods plague thee, for thou art

a man! if thou dost perform, confound thee, for

thou art a man!

ALCIBIADES

I have heard in some sort of thy miseries.

TIMON

Thou saw'st them, when I had prosperity.

ALCIBIADES

I see them now; then was a blessed time.

TIMON

As thine is now, held with a brace of harlots.

TIMANDRA

Is this the Athenian minion, whom the world

Voiced so regardfully?

TIMON

Art thou Timandra?

TIMANDRA

Yes.

TIMON

Be a whore still: they love thee not that use thee;

Give them diseases, leaving with thee their lust.

Make use of thy salt hours: season the slaves

For tubs and baths; bring down rose-cheeked youth

To the tub-fast and the diet.

TIMANDRA

Hang thee, monster!

ALCIBIADES

Pardon him, sweet Timandra; for his wits

Are drown'd and lost in his calamities.

I have but little gold of late, brave Timon,

The want whereof doth daily make revolt

In my penurious band: I have heard, and grieved,

How cursed Athens, mindless of thy worth,

Forgetting thy great deeds, when neighbour states,

But for thy sword and fortune, trod upon them,--

TIMON

I prithee, beat thy drum, and get thee gone.

ALCIBIADES

I am thy friend, and pity thee, dear Timon.

TIMON

How dost thou pity him whom thou dost trouble?

I had rather be alone.

ALCIBIADES

Why, fare thee well:

Here is some gold for thee.

TIMON

Keep it, I cannot eat it.

ALCIBIADES

When I have laid proud Athens on a heap,--

TIMON

Warr'st thou 'gainst Athens?

ALCIBIADES

Ay, Timon, and have cause.

TIMON

The gods confound them all in thy conquest;

And thee after, when thou hast conquer'd!

ALCIBIADES

Why me, Timon?

TIMON

That, by killing of villains,

Thou wast born to conquer my country.

Put up thy gold: go on,--here's gold,--go on;

Be as a planetary plague, when Jove

Will o'er some high-viced city hang his poison

In the sick air: let not thy sword skip one:

Pity not honour'd age for his white beard;

He is an usurer: strike me the counterfeit matron;

It is her habit only that is honest,

Herself's a bawd: let not the virgin's cheek

Make soft thy trenchant sword; for those milk-paps,

That through the window-bars bore at men's eyes,

Are not within the leaf of pity writ,

But set them down horrible traitors: spare not the babe,

Whose dimpled smiles from fools exhaust their mercy;

Think it a bastard, whom the oracle

Hath doubtfully pronounced thy throat shall cut,

And mince it sans remorse: swear against objects;

Put armour on thine ears and on thine eyes;

Whose proof, nor yells of mothers, maids, nor babes,

Nor sight of priests in holy vestments bleeding,

Shall pierce a jot. There's gold to pay soldiers:

Make large confusion; and, thy fury spent,

Confounded be thyself! Speak not, be gone.

ALCIBIADES

Hast thou gold yet? I'll take the gold thou

givest me,

Not all thy counsel.

TIMON

Dost thou, or dost thou not, heaven's curse

upon thee!

PHRYNIATIMANDRA

Give us some gold, good Timon: hast thou more?

TIMON

Enough to make a whore forswear her trade,

And to make whores, a bawd. Hold up, you sluts,

Your aprons mountant: you are not oathable,

Although, I know, you 'll swear, terribly swear

Into strong shudders and to heavenly agues

The immortal gods that hear you,--spare your oaths,

I'll trust to your conditions: be whores still;

And he whose pious breath seeks to convert you,

Be strong in whore, allure him, burn him up;

Let your close fire predominate his smoke,

And be no turncoats: yet may your pains, six months,

Be quite contrary: and thatch your poor thin roofs

With burthens of the dead;--some that were hang'd,

No matter:--wear them, betray with them: whore still;

Paint till a horse may mire upon your face,

A pox of wrinkles!

PHRYNIATIMANDRA

Well, more gold: what then?

Believe't, that we'll do any thing for gold.

TIMON

Consumptions sow

In hollow bones of man; strike their sharp shins,

And mar men's spurring. Crack the lawyer's voice,

That he may never more false title plead,

Nor sound his quillets shrilly: hoar the flamen,

That scolds against the quality of flesh,

And not believes himself: down with the nose,

Down with it flat; take the bridge quite away

Of him that, his particular to foresee,

Smells from the general weal: make curl'd-pate

ruffians bald;

And let the unscarr'd braggarts of the war

Derive some pain from you: plague all;

That your activity may defeat and quell

The source of all erection. There's more gold:

Do you damn others, and let this damn you,

And ditches grave you all!

PHRYNIATIMANDRA

More counsel with more money, bounteous Timon.

TIMON

More whore, more mischief first; I have given you earnest.

ALCIBIADES

Strike up the drum towards Athens! Farewell, Timon:

If I thrive well, I'll visit thee again.

TIMON

If I hope well, I'll never see thee more.

ALCIBIADES

I never did thee harm.

TIMON

Yes, thou spokest well of me.

ALCIBIADES

Call'st thou that harm?

TIMON

Men daily find it. Get thee away, and take

Thy beagles with thee.

ALCIBIADES

We but offend him. Strike!

Drum beats.

    *Exeunt ALCIBIADES, PHRYNIA, and TIMANDRA*

TIMON

That nature, being sick of man's unkindness,

Should yet be hungry! Common mother, thou,

Digging

Whose womb unmeasurable, and infinite breast,

Teems, and feeds all; whose self-same mettle,

Whereof thy proud child, arrogant man, is puff'd,

Engenders the black toad and adder blue,

The gilded newt and eyeless venom'd worm,

With all the abhorred births below crisp heaven

Whereon Hyperion's quickening fire doth shine;

Yield him, who all thy human sons doth hate,

From forth thy plenteous bosom, one poor root!

Ensear thy fertile and conceptious womb,

Let it no more bring out ingrateful man!

Go great with tigers, dragons, wolves, and bears;

Teem with new monsters, whom thy upward face

Hath to the marbled mansion all above

Never presented!--O, a root,--dear thanks!--

Dry up thy marrows, vines, and plough-torn leas;

Whereof ungrateful man, with liquorish draughts

And morsels unctuous, greases his pure mind,

That from it all consideration slips!

*Enter APEMANTUS*

More man? plague, plague!

APEMANTUS

I was directed hither: men report

Thou dost affect my manners, and dost use them.

TIMON

'Tis, then, because thou dost not keep a dog,

Whom I would imitate: consumption catch thee!

APEMANTUS

This is in thee a nature but infected;

A poor unmanly melancholy sprung

From change of fortune. Why this spade? this place?

This slave-like habit? and these looks of care?

Thy flatterers yet wear silk, drink wine, lie soft;

Hug their diseased perfumes, and have forgot

That ever Timon was. Shame not these woods,

By putting on the cunning of a carper.

Be thou a flatterer now, and seek to thrive

By that which has undone thee: hinge thy knee,

And let his very breath, whom thou'lt observe,

Blow off thy cap; praise his most vicious strain,

And call it excellent: thou wast told thus;

Thou gavest thine ears like tapsters that bid welcome

To knaves and all approachers: 'tis most just

That thou turn rascal; hadst thou wealth again,

Rascals should have 't. Do not assume my likeness.

TIMON

Were I like thee, I'ld throw away myself.

APEMANTUS

Thou hast cast away thyself, being like thyself;

A madman so long, now a fool. What, think'st

That the bleak air, thy boisterous chamberlain,

Will put thy shirt on warm? will these moss'd trees,

That have outlived the eagle, page thy heels,

And skip where thou point'st out? will the

cold brook,

Candied with ice, caudle thy morning taste,

To cure thy o'er-night's surfeit? Call the creatures

Whose naked natures live in an the spite

Of wreakful heaven, whose bare unhoused trunks,

To the conflicting elements exposed,

Answer mere nature; bid them flatter thee;

O, thou shalt find--

TIMON

A fool of thee: depart.

APEMANTUS

I love thee better now than e'er I did.

TIMON

I hate thee worse.

APEMANTUS

Why?

TIMON

Thou flatter'st misery.

APEMANTUS

I flatter not; but say thou art a caitiff.

TIMON

Why dost thou seek me out?

APEMANTUS

To vex thee.

TIMON

Always a villain's office or a fool's.

Dost please thyself in't?

APEMANTUS

Ay.

TIMON

What! a knave too?

APEMANTUS

If thou didst put this sour-cold habit on

To castigate thy pride, 'twere well: but thou

Dost it enforcedly; thou'ldst courtier be again,

Wert thou not beggar. Willing misery

Outlives encertain pomp, is crown'd before:

The one is filling still, never complete;

The other, at high wish: best state, contentless,

Hath a distracted and most wretched being,

Worse than the worst, content.

Thou shouldst desire to die, being miserable.

TIMON

Not by his breath that is more miserable.

Thou art a slave, whom Fortune's tender arm

With favour never clasp'd; but bred a dog.

Hadst thou, like us from our first swath, proceeded

The sweet degrees that this brief world affords

To such as may the passive drugs of it

Freely command, thou wouldst have plunged thyself

In general riot; melted down thy youth

In different beds of lust; and never learn'd

The icy precepts of respect, but follow'd

The sugar'd game before thee. But myself,

Who had the world as my confectionary,

The mouths, the tongues, the eyes and hearts of men

At duty, more than I could frame employment,

That numberless upon me stuck as leaves

Do on the oak, hive with one winter's brush

Fell from their boughs and left me open, bare

For every storm that blows: I, to bear this,

That never knew but better, is some burden:

Thy nature did commence in sufferance, time

Hath made thee hard in't. Why shouldst thou hate men?

They never flatter'd thee: what hast thou given?

If thou wilt curse, thy father, that poor rag,

Must be thy subject, who in spite put stuff

To some she beggar and compounded thee

Poor rogue hereditary. Hence, be gone!

If thou hadst not been born the worst of men,

Thou hadst been a knave and flatterer.

APEMANTUS

Art thou proud yet?

TIMON

Ay, that I am not thee.

APEMANTUS

I, that I was

No prodigal.

TIMON

I, that I am one now:

Were all the wealth I have shut up in thee,

I'ld give thee leave to hang it. Get thee gone.

That the whole life of Athens were in this!

Thus would I eat it.

Eating a root

APEMANTUS

Here; I will mend thy feast.

Offering him a root

TIMON

First mend my company, take away thyself.

APEMANTUS

So I shall mend mine own, by the lack of thine.

TIMON

'Tis not well mended so, it is but botch'd;

if not, I would it were.

APEMANTUS

What wouldst thou have to Athens?

TIMON

Thee thither in a whirlwind. If thou wilt,

Tell them there I have gold; look, so I have.

APEMANTUS

Here is no use for gold.

TIMON

The best and truest;

For here it sleeps, and does no hired harm.

APEMANTUS

Where liest o' nights, Timon?

TIMON

Under that's above me.

Where feed'st thou o' days, Apemantus?

APEMANTUS

Where my stomach finds meat; or, rather, where I eat
it.

TIMON

Would poison were obedient and knew my mind!

APEMANTUS

Where wouldst thou send it?

TIMON

To sauce thy dishes.

APEMANTUS

The middle of humanity thou never knewest, but the
extremity of both ends: when thou wast in thy gilt
and thy perfume, they mocked thee for too much
curiosity; in thy rags thou knowest none, but art
despised for the contrary. There's a medlar for
thee, eat it.

TIMON

On what I hate I feed not.

APEMANTUS

Dost hate a medlar?

TIMON

Ay, though it look like thee.

APEMANTUS

An thou hadst hated meddlers sooner, thou shouldst
have loved thyself better now. What man didst thou
ever know unthrift that was beloved after his means?

TIMON

Who, without those means thou talkest of, didst thou
ever know beloved?

APEMANTUS

Myself.

TIMON

I understand thee; thou hadst some means to keep a
dog.

APEMANTUS

What things in the world canst thou nearest compare
to thy flatterers?

TIMON

Women nearest; but men, men are the things
themselves. What wouldst thou do with the world,
Apemantus, if it lay in thy power?

APEMANTUS

Give it the beasts, to be rid of the men.

TIMON

Wouldst thou have thyself fall in the confusion of
men, and remain a beast with the beasts?

APEMANTUS

Ay, Timon.

TIMON

A beastly ambition, which the gods grant thee t'
attain to! If thou wert the lion, the fox would
beguile thee; if thou wert the lamb, the fox would
eat three: if thou wert the fox, the lion would

suspect thee, when peradventure thou wert accused by
the ass: if thou wert the ass, thy dulness would
torment thee, and still thou livedst but as a
breakfast to the wolf: if thou wert the wolf, thy
greediness would afflict thee, and oft thou shouldst
hazard thy life for thy dinner: wert thou the
unicorn, pride and wrath would confound thee and
make thine own self the conquest of thy fury: wert
thou a bear, thou wouldst be killed by the horse:
wert thou a horse, thou wouldst be seized by the
leopard: wert thou a leopard, thou wert german to
the lion and the spots of thy kindred were jurors on
thy life: all thy safety were remotion and thy
defence absence. What beast couldst thou be, that
were not subject to a beast? and what a beast art
thou already, that seest not thy loss in
transformation!

APEMANTUS

If thou couldst please me with speaking to me, thou
mightst have hit upon it here: the commonwealth of
Athens is become a forest of beasts.

TIMON

How has the ass broke the wall, that thou art out of the city?

APEMANTUS

Yonder comes a poet and a painter: the plague of
company light upon thee! I will fear to catch it
and give way: when I know not what else to do, I'll

see thee again.

TIMON

When there is nothing living but thee, thou shalt be

welcome. I had rather be a beggar's dog than Apemantus.

APEMANTUS

Thou art the cap of all the fools alive.

TIMON

Would thou wert clean enough to spit upon!

APEMANTUS

A plague on thee! thou art too bad to curse.

TIMON

All villains that do stand by thee are pure.

APEMANTUS

There is no leprosy but what thou speak'st.

TIMON

If I name thee.

I'll beat thee, but I should infect my hands.

APEMANTUS

I would my tongue could rot them off!

TIMON

Away, thou issue of a mangy dog!

Choler does kill me that thou art alive;

I swound to see thee.

APEMANTUS

Would thou wouldst burst!

TIMON

Away,

Thou tedious rogue! I am sorry I shall lose

A stone by thee.

Throws a stone at him

APEMANTUS

Beast!

TIMON

Slave!

APEMANTUS

Toad!

TIMON

Rogue, rogue, rogue!

I am sick of this false world, and will love nought

But even the mere necessities upon 't.

Then, Timon, presently prepare thy grave;

Lie where the light foam the sea may beat

Thy grave-stone daily: make thine epitaph,

That death in me at others' lives may laugh.

To the gold

O thou sweet king-killer, and dear divorce

'Twixt natural son and sire! thou bright defiler

Of Hymen's purest bed! thou valiant Mars!

Thou ever young, fresh, loved and delicate wooer,

Whose blush doth thaw the consecrated snow

That lies on Dian's lap! thou visible god,

That solder'st close impossibilities,

And makest them kiss! that speak'st with

every tongue,

To every purpose! O thou touch of hearts!

Think, thy slave man rebels, and by thy virtue

Set them into confounding odds, that beasts

May have the world in empire!

APEMANTUS

Would 'twere so!

But not till I am dead. I'll say thou'st gold:

Thou wilt be throng'd to shortly.

TIMON

Throng'd to!

APEMANTUS

Ay.

TIMON

Thy back, I prithee.

APEMANTUS

Live, and love thy misery.

TIMON

Long live so, and so die.

    *Exit APEMANTUS*

I am quit.

Moe things like men! Eat, Timon, and abhor them.

    *Enter Banditti*

First Bandit

Where should he have this gold? It is some poor

fragment, some slender sort of his remainder: the

mere want of gold, and the falling-from of his

friends, drove him into this melancholy.

**Second Bandit**

It is noised he hath a mass of treasure.

**Third Bandit**

Let us make the assay upon him: if he care not
for't, he will supply us easily; if he covetously
reserve it, how shall's get it?

**Second Bandit**

True; for he bears it not about him, 'tis hid.

**First Bandit**

Is not this he?

**Banditti**

Where?

**Second Bandit**

'Tis his description.

**Third Bandit**

He; I know him.

**Banditti**

Save thee, Timon.

**TIMON**

Now, thieves?

**Banditti**

Soldiers, not thieves.

**TIMON**

Both too; and women's sons.

**Banditti**

We are not thieves, but men that much do want.

**TIMON**

Your greatest want is, you want much of meat.

Why should you want? Behold, the earth hath roots;

Within this mile break forth a hundred springs;

The oaks bear mast, the briers scarlet hips;

The bounteous housewife, nature, on each bush

Lays her full mess before you. Want! why want?

First Bandit

We cannot live on grass, on berries, water,

As beasts and birds and fishes.

TIMON

Nor on the beasts themselves, the birds, and fishes;

You must eat men. Yet thanks I must you con

That you are thieves profess'd, that you work not

In holier shapes: for there is boundless theft

In limited professions. Rascal thieves,

Here's gold. Go, suck the subtle blood o' the grape,

Till the high fever seethe your blood to froth,

And so 'scape hanging: trust not the physician;

His antidotes are poison, and he slays

Moe than you rob: take wealth and lives together;

Do villany, do, since you protest to do't,

Like workmen. I'll example you with thievery.

The sun's a thief, and with his great attraction

Robs the vast sea: the moon's an arrant thief,

And her pale fire she snatches from the sun:

The sea's a thief, whose liquid surge resolves

The moon into salt tears: the earth's a thief,

That feeds and breeds by a composture stolen

From general excrement: each thing's a thief:

The laws, your curb and whip, in their rough power

Have uncheque'd theft. Love not yourselves: away,

Rob one another. There's more gold. Cut throats:

All that you meet are thieves: to Athens go,

Break open shops; nothing can you steal,

But thieves do lose it: steal no less for this

I give you; and gold confound you howsoe'er! Amen.

Third Bandit

Has almost charmed me from my profession, by

persuading me to it.

First Bandit

'Tis in the malice of mankind that he thus advises

us; not to have us thrive in our mystery.

Second Bandit

I'll believe him as an enemy, and give over my trade.

First Bandit

Let us first see peace in Athens: there is no time

so miserable but a man may be true.

*Exeunt Banditti*

*Enter FLAVIUS*

FLAVIUS

O you gods!

Is yond despised and ruinous man my lord?

Full of decay and failing? O monument

And wonder of good deeds evilly bestow'd!

What an alteration of honour

Has desperate want made!

What viler thing upon the earth than friends

Who can bring noblest minds to basest ends!

How rarely does it meet with this time's guise,

When man was wish'd to love his enemies!

Grant I may ever love, and rather woo

Those that would mischief me than those that do!

Has caught me in his eye: I will present

My honest grief unto him; and, as my lord,

Still serve him with my life. My dearest master!

TIMON

Away! what art thou?

FLAVIUS

Have you forgot me, sir?

TIMON

Why dost ask that? I have forgot all men;

Then, if thou grant'st thou'rt a man, I have forgot thee.

FLAVIUS

An honest poor servant of yours.

TIMON

Then I know thee not:

I never had honest man about me, I; all

I kept were knaves, to serve in meat to villains.

FLAVIUS

The gods are witness,

Ne'er did poor steward wear a truer grief

For his undone lord than mine eyes for you.

TIMON

What, dost thou weep? Come nearer. Then I
love thee,

Because thou art a woman, and disclaim'st

Flinty mankind; whose eyes do never give

But thorough lust and laughter. Pity's sleeping:

Strange times, that weep with laughing, not with weeping!

FLAVIUS

I beg of you to know me, good my lord,

To accept my grief and whilst this poor wealth lasts

To entertain me as your steward still.

TIMON

Had I a steward

So true, so just, and now so comfortable?

It almost turns my dangerous nature mild.

Let me behold thy face. Surely, this man

Was born of woman.

Forgive my general and exceptless rashness,

You perpetual-sober gods! I do proclaim

One honest man--mistake me not--but one;

No more, I pray,--and he's a steward.

How fain would I have hated all mankind!

And thou redeem'st thyself: but all, save thee,

I fell with curses.

Methinks thou art more honest now than wise;

For, by oppressing and betraying me,

Thou mightst have sooner got another service:

For many so arrive at second masters,

Upon their first lord's neck. But tell me true--

For I must ever doubt, though ne'er so sure--

Is not thy kindness subtle, covetous,

If not a usuring kindness, and, as rich men deal gifts,

Expecting in return twenty for one?

FLAVIUS

No, my most worthy master; in whose breast

Doubt and suspect, alas, are placed too late:

You should have fear'd false times when you did feast:

Suspect still comes where an estate is least.

That which I show, heaven knows, is merely love,

Duty and zeal to your unmatched mind,

Care of your food and living; and, believe it,

My most honour'd lord,

For any benefit that points to me,

Either in hope or present, I'ld exchange

For this one wish, that you had power and wealth

To requite me, by making rich yourself.

TIMON

Look thee, 'tis so! Thou singly honest man,

Here, take: the gods out of my misery

Have sent thee treasure. Go, live rich and happy;

But thus condition'd: thou shalt build from men;

Hate all, curse all, show charity to none,

But let the famish'd flesh slide from the bone,

Ere thou relieve the beggar; give to dogs

What thou deny'st to men; let prisons swallow 'em,

Debts wither 'em to nothing; be men like

blasted woods,

And may diseases lick up their false bloods!

And so farewell and thrive.

FLAVIUS

O, let me stay,

And comfort you, my master.

TIMON

If thou hatest curses,

Stay not; fly, whilst thou art blest and free:

Ne'er see thou man, and let me ne'er see thee.

*Exit FLAVIUS. TIMON retires to his cave*


# ACT V

## SCENE I. The woods. Before Timon's cave.

*Enter Poet and Painter; TIMON watching them from his cave*

Painter

As I took note of the place, it cannot be far where

he abides.

Poet

What's to be thought of him? does the rumour hold

for true, that he's so full of gold?

Painter

Certain: Alcibiades reports it; Phrynia and

Timandra had gold of him: he likewise enriched poor

straggling soldiers with great quantity: 'tis said

he gave unto his steward a mighty sum.

Poet

Then this breaking of his has been but a try for his friends.

Painter

Nothing else: you shall see him a palm in Athens

again, and flourish with the highest. Therefore

'tis not amiss we tender our loves to him, in this

supposed distress of his: it will show honestly in

us; and is very likely to load our purposes with

what they travail for, if it be a just true report

that goes of his having.

Poet

What have you now to present unto him?

Painter

Nothing at this time but my visitation: only I will

promise him an excellent piece.

Poet

I must serve him so too, tell him of an intent

that's coming toward him.

Painter

Good as the best. Promising is the very air o' the

time: it opens the eyes of expectation:

performance is ever the duller for his act; and,

but in the plainer and simpler kind of people, the

deed of saying is quite out of use. To promise is

most courtly and fashionable: performance is a kind

of will or testament which argues a great sickness

in his judgment that makes it.

TIMON comes from his cave, behind

TIMON

[Aside] Excellent workman! thou canst not paint a

man so bad as is thyself.

Poet

I am thinking what I shall say I have provided for

him: it must be a personating of himself; a satire

against the softness of prosperity, with a discovery

of the infinite flatteries that follow youth and opulency.

TIMON

[Aside] Must thou needs stand for a villain in

thine own work? wilt thou whip thine own faults in

other men? Do so, I have gold for thee.

Poet

Nay, let's seek him:

Then do we sin against our own estate,

When we may profit meet, and come too late.

Painter

True;

When the day serves, before black-corner'd night,

Find what thou want'st by free and offer'd light. Come.

TIMON

[Aside] I'll meet you at the turn. What a

god's gold,

That he is worshipp'd in a baser temple

Than where swine feed!

'Tis thou that rigg'st the bark and plough'st the foam,

Settlest admired reverence in a slave:

To thee be worship! and thy saints for aye

Be crown'd with plagues that thee alone obey!

Fit I meet them.

Coming forward

Poet

Hail, worthy Timon!

Painter

Our late noble master!

TIMON

Have I once lived to see two honest men?

Poet

Sir,

Having often of your open bounty tasted,

Hearing you were retired, your friends fall'n off,

Whose thankless natures--O abhorred spirits!--

Not all the whips of heaven are large enough:

What! to you,

Whose star-like nobleness gave life and influence

To their whole being! I am rapt and cannot cover

The monstrous bulk of this ingratitude

With any size of words.

TIMON

Let it go naked, men may see't the better:

You that are honest, by being what you are,

Make them best seen and known.

Painter

He and myself

Have travail'd in the great shower of your gifts,

And sweetly felt it.

TIMON

Ay, you are honest men.

Painter

We are hither come to offer you our service.

TIMON

Most honest men! Why, how shall I requite you?

Can you eat roots, and drink cold water? no.

Both

What we can do, we'll do, to do you service.

TIMON

Ye're honest men: ye've heard that I have gold;

I am sure you have: speak truth; ye're honest men.

Painter

So it is said, my noble lord; but therefore

Came not my friend nor I.

TIMON

Good honest men! Thou draw'st a counterfeit

Best in all Athens: thou'rt, indeed, the best;

Thou counterfeit'st most lively.

Painter

So, so, my lord.

TIMON

E'en so, sir, as I say. And, for thy fiction,

Why, thy verse swells with stuff so fine and smooth

That thou art even natural in thine art.

But, for all this, my honest-natured friends,

I must needs say you have a little fault:

Marry, 'tis not monstrous in you, neither wish I

You take much pains to mend.

Both

Beseech your honour

To make it known to us.

TIMON

You'll take it ill.

Both

Most thankfully, my lord.

TIMON

Will you, indeed?

Both

Doubt it not, worthy lord.

TIMON

There's never a one of you but trusts a knave,

That mightily deceives you.

Both

Do we, my lord?

TIMON

Ay, and you hear him cog, see him dissemble,

Know his gross patchery, love him, feed him,

Keep in your bosom: yet remain assured

That he's a made-up villain.

Painter

I know none such, my lord.

Poet

Nor I.

TIMON

Look you, I love you well; I'll give you gold,

Rid me these villains from your companies:

Hang them or stab them, drown them in a draught,

Confound them by some course, and come to me,

I'll give you gold enough.

Both

Name them, my lord, let's know them.

TIMON

You that way and you this, but two in company;

Each man apart, all single and alone,

Yet an arch-villain keeps him company.

If where thou art two villains shall not be,

Come not near him. If thou wouldst not reside

But where one villain is, then him abandon.

Hence, pack! there's gold; you came for gold, ye slaves:

To Painter

You have work'd for me; there's payment for you: hence!

To Poet

You are an alchemist; make gold of that.

Out, rascal dogs!

Beats them out, and then retires to his cave

*Enter FLAVIUS and two Senators*

FLAVIUS

It is in vain that you would speak with Timon;

For he is set so only to himself

That nothing but himself which looks like man

Is friendly with him.

First Senator

Bring us to his cave:

It is our part and promise to the Athenians

To speak with Timon.

Second Senator

At all times alike

Men are not still the same: 'twas time and griefs

That framed him thus: time, with his fairer hand,

Offering the fortunes of his former days,

The former man may make him. Bring us to him,

And chance it as it may.

FLAVIUS

Here is his cave.

Peace and content be here! Lord Timon! Timon!

Look out, and speak to friends: the Athenians,

By two of their most reverend senate, greet thee:

Speak to them, noble Timon.

TIMON comes from his cave

TIMON

Thou sun, that comfort'st, burn! Speak, and

be hang'd:

For each true word, a blister! and each false

Be as cauterizing to the root o' the tongue,

Consuming it with speaking!

First Senator

Worthy Timon,--

TIMON

Of none but such as you, and you of Timon.

First Senator

The senators of Athens greet thee, Timon.

TIMON

I thank them; and would send them back the plague,

Could I but catch it for them.

First Senator

O, forget

What we are sorry for ourselves in thee.

The senators with one consent of love

Entreat thee back to Athens; who have thought

On special dignities, which vacant lie

For thy best use and wearing.

Second Senator

They confess

Toward thee forgetfulness too general, gross:

Which now the public body, which doth seldom

Play the recanter, feeling in itself

A lack of Timon's aid, hath sense withal

Of its own fail, restraining aid to Timon;

And send forth us, to make their sorrow'd render,

Together with a recompense more fruitful

Than their offence can weigh down by the dram;

Ay, even such heaps and sums of love and wealth

As shall to thee blot out what wrongs were theirs

And write in thee the figures of their love,

Ever to read them thine.

TIMON

You witch me in it;

Surprise me to the very brink of tears:

Lend me a fool's heart and a woman's eyes,

And I'll beweep these comforts, worthy senators.

First Senator

Therefore, so please thee to return with us

And of our Athens, thine and ours, to take

The captainship, thou shalt be met with thanks,

Allow'd with absolute power and thy good name

Live with authority: so soon we shall drive back

Of Alcibiades the approaches wild,

Who, like a boar too savage, doth root up

His country's peace.

Second Senator

And shakes his threatening sword

Against the walls of Athens.

First Senator

Therefore, Timon,--

TIMON

Well, sir, I will; therefore, I will, sir; thus:

If Alcibiades kill my countrymen,

Let Alcibiades know this of Timon,

That Timon cares not. But if be sack fair Athens,

And take our goodly aged men by the beards,

Giving our holy virgins to the stain

Of contumelious, beastly, mad-brain'd war,

Then let him know, and tell him Timon speaks it,

In pity of our aged and our youth,

I cannot choose but tell him, that I care not,

And let him take't at worst; for their knives care not,

While you have throats to answer: for myself,

There's not a whittle in the unruly camp

But I do prize it at my love before

The reverend'st throat in Athens. So I leave you

To the protection of the prosperous gods,

As thieves to keepers.

FLAVIUS

Stay not, all's in vain.

TIMON

Why, I was writing of my epitaph;

it will be seen to-morrow: my long sickness

Of health and living now begins to mend,

And nothing brings me all things. Go, live still;

Be Alcibiades your plague, you his,

And last so long enough!

First Senator

We speak in vain.

TIMON

But yet I love my country, and am not

One that rejoices in the common wreck,

As common bruit doth put it.

First Senator

That's well spoke.

TIMON

Commend me to my loving countrymen,--

First Senator

These words become your lips as they pass

thorough them.

Second Senator

And enter in our ears like great triumphers

In their applauding gates.

TIMON

Commend me to them,

And tell them that, to ease them of their griefs,

Their fears of hostile strokes, their aches, losses,

Their pangs of love, with other incident throes

That nature's fragile vessel doth sustain

In life's uncertain voyage, I will some kindness do them:

I'll teach them to prevent wild Alcibiades' wrath.

First Senator

I like this well; he will return again.

TIMON

I have a tree, which grows here in my close,

That mine own use invites me to cut down,

And shortly must I fell it: tell my friends,

Tell Athens, in the sequence of degree

From high to low throughout, that whoso please

To stop affliction, let him take his haste,

Come hither, ere my tree hath felt the axe,

And hang himself. I pray you, do my greeting.

FLAVIUS

Trouble him no further; thus you still shall find him.

TIMON

Come not to me again: but say to Athens,

Timon hath made his everlasting mansion

Upon the beached verge of the salt flood;

Who once a day with his embossed froth

The turbulent surge shall cover: thither come,

And let my grave-stone be your oracle.

Lips, let sour words go by and language end:

What is amiss plague and infection mend!

Graves only be men's works and death their gain!

Sun, hide thy beams! Timon hath done his reign.

Retires to his cave

First Senator

His discontents are unremoveably

Coupled to nature.

Second Senator

Our hope in him is dead: let us return,

And strain what other means is left unto us

In our dear peril.

First Senator

It requires swift foot.

*Exeunt*

## SCENE II. Before the walls of Athens.

*Enter two Senators and a Messenger*

First Senator

Thou hast painfully discover'd: are his files

As full as thy report?

Messenger

have spoke the least:

Besides, his expedition promises

Present approach.

Second Senator

We stand much hazard, if they bring not Timon.

Messenger

I met a courier, one mine ancient friend;

Whom, though in general part we were opposed,

Yet our old love made a particular force,

And made us speak like friends: this man was riding

From Alcibiades to Timon's cave,

With letters of entreaty, which imported

His fellowship i' the cause against your city,

In part for his sake moved.

First Senator

Here come our brothers.

*Enter the Senators from TIMON*

Third Senator

No talk of Timon, nothing of him expect.

The enemies' drum is heard, and fearful scouring

Doth choke the air with dust: in, and prepare:

Ours is the fall, I fear; our foes the snare.

*Exeunt*

## SCENE III. The woods. Timon's cave, and a rude tomb seen.

*Enter a Soldier, seeking TIMON*

Soldier

By all description this should be the place.

Who's here? speak, ho! No answer! What is this?

Timon is dead, who hath outstretch'd his span:

Some beast rear'd this; there does not live a man.

Dead, sure; and this his grave. What's on this tomb

I cannot read; the character I'll take with wax:

Our captain hath in every figure skill,

An aged interpreter, though young in days:

Before proud Athens he's set down by this,

Whose fall the mark of his ambition is.

*Exit*

## SCENE IV. Before the walls of Athens.

Trumpets sound.

*Enter ALCIBIADES with his powers*

ALCIBIADES

Sound to this coward and lascivious town

Our terrible approach.

A parley sounded

*Enter Senators on the walls*

Till now you have gone on and fill'd the time

With all licentious measure, making your wills

The scope of justice; till now myself and such

As slept within the shadow of your power

Hav e wander'd with our traversed arms and breathed

Our sufferance vainly: now the time is flush,

When crouching marrow in the bearer strong

Cries of itself 'No more:' now breathless wrong

Shall sit and pant in your great chairs of ease,

And pursy insolence shall break his wind

With fear and horrid flight.

First Senator

Noble and young,

When thy first griefs were but a mere conceit,

Ere thou hadst power or we had cause of fear,

We sent to thee, to give thy rages balm,

To wipe out our ingratitude with loves

Above their quantity.

Second Senator

So did we woo

Transformed Timon to our city's love

By humble message and by promised means:

We were not all unkind, nor all deserve

The common stroke of war.

First Senator

These walls of ours

Were not erected by their hands from whom

You have received your griefs; nor are they such

That these great towers, trophies and schools

should fall

For private faults in them.

Second Senator

Nor are they living

Who were the motives that you first went out;

Shame that they wanted cunning, in excess

Hath broke their hearts. March, noble lord,

Into our city with thy banners spread:

By decimation, and a tithed death--

If thy revenges hunger for that food

Which nature loathes--take thou the destined tenth,

And by the hazard of the spotted die

Let die the spotted.

First Senator

All have not offended;

For those that were, it is not square to take

On those that are, revenges: crimes, like lands,

Are not inherited. Then, dear countryman,

Bring in thy ranks, but leave without thy rage:

Spare thy Athenian cradle and those kin

Which in the bluster of thy wrath must fall

With those that have offended: like a shepherd,

Approach the fold and cull the infected forth,

But kill not all together.

Second Senator

What thou wilt,

Thou rather shalt enforce it with thy smile

Than hew to't with thy sword.

First Senator

Set but thy foot

Against our rampired gates, and they shall ope;

So thou wilt send thy gentle heart before,

To say thou'lt enter friendly.

Second Senator

Throw thy glove,

Or any token of thine honour else,

That thou wilt use the wars as thy redress

And not as our confusion, all thy powers

Shall make their harbour in our town, till we

Have seal'd thy full desire.

ALCIBIADES

Then there's my glove;

Descend, and open your uncharged ports:

Those enemies of Timon's and mine own

Whom you yourselves shall set out for reproof

Fall and no more: and, to atone your fears

With my more noble meaning, not a man

Shall pass his quarter, or offend the stream

Of regular justice in your city's bounds,

But shall be render'd to your public laws

At heaviest answer.

Both

'Tis most nobly spoken.

ALCIBIADES

Descend, and keep your words.

The Senators descend, and open the gates

*Enter Soldier*

Soldier

My noble general, Timon is dead;

Entomb'd upon the very hem o' the sea;

And on his grave-stone this insculpture, which

With wax I brought away, whose soft impression

Interprets for my poor ignorance.

ALCIBIADES

[Reads the epitaph] 'Here lies a

wretched corse, of wretched soul bereft:

Seek not my name: a plague consume you wicked

caitiffs left!

Here lie I, Timon; who, alive, all living men did hate:

Pass by and curse thy fill, but pass and stay

not here thy gait.'

These well express in thee thy latter spirits:

Though thou abhorr'dst in us our human griefs,

Scorn'dst our brain's flow and those our

droplets which

From niggard nature fall, yet rich conceit

Taught thee to make vast Neptune weep for aye

On thy low grave, on faults forgiven. Dead

Is noble Timon: of whose memory

Hereafter more. Bring me into your city,

And I will use the olive with my sword,

Make war breed peace, make peace stint war, make each

Prescribe to other as each other's leech.

Let our drums strike.

*Exeunt*

*Finis*

**THE ACTORS NAMES.**
TYMON of Athens.
Lucius, And Lucullus, two Flattering Lords.
Appemantus, a Churlish Philosopher.
Sempronius another flattering Lord.
Alcibiades, an Athenian Captaine.
Poet.
Painter.
Ieweller.
Merchant.
Certaine Theeues.
Flaminius, one of Tymons Seruants.
Seruilius, another.
Caphis.
Varro.
Philo.
Titus.
Lucius.
Hortensis Seuerall Seruants to Vsurers.
Ventigius. one of Tymons false Friends.
Cupid.
Sempronius. With diuers other Seruants, And Attendants.

**THE LIFE OF TYMON OF ATHENS.**

CPSIA information can be obtained
at www.ICGtesting.com
Printed in the USA
BVHW031402231020
591690BV00001B/174